❧ THE DYNAMICS OF GERMAN INDUSTRY ❧

MAKING SENSE OF HISTORY
Studies in Historical Cultures
General Editor: Jörn Rüsen, in Association with Christian Geulen

The Dynamics of German Industry
Germany's Path toward the New Economy and the American Challenge

Werner Abelshauser

Berghahn Books
New York • Oxford

First published in 2005 by

Berghahn Books

www.BerghahnBooks.com

© 2005 Werner Abelshauser

Library of Congress Cataloging-in-Publication Data

The dynamics of German Industry : Germany's path toward the new economy and the
American challenge / Werner Abelshauser; translated by David R. Antal.
    p. cm.
  Includes bibliographical references and index.
  ISBN 1-84545-072-8
   1. Germany--Economic conditions. 2. Germany--Social conditions. 3. Industrial
organization--Germany. 4. Industrial organization--United States. I. Abelshauser, Werner.

HC283.D94 2005
338.0943--dc22   2005042010

British Library Cataloguing in Publication Data
A catalogue record for this book is available
from the British Library.

Printed in Canada

Contents

III. The German Production Regime

IV. The German Road to the Twenty-first Century

List of Figures and Tables

Introduction

This outline of Germany's path to the postindustrial economy asks a good deal of its readers. It calls upon them to try and understand the world through a radically new economic worldview. The foil for explaining current economic interaction is not the familiar Industrial Revolution of the late eighteenth century, but rather what economist Douglass C. North calls the Second Economic Revolution, which closed the modern era at the end of the nineteenth century and inaugurated the period of nonmaterial production. Although the theoretical foundations of this paradigm have set sufficiently in the two decades since they were laid, studies substantiating these new insights with the empirical authority of historical analysis are still rare.

Germany lends itself particularly well to an inquiry into the implications of this fresh viewpoint's two meanings. For one thing, the new perspective compels one to redecipher the riddle of German economic history now that research has long rejected the notion that Germany took a "special path" to the modern age. For another, it provides a new angle from which the economic challenges of the present can be understood and placed in historical context. If divorced from this historical dimension, attempts to shape the institutions of the New Economy are bound to fail. Above all, however, Germany's economic history can demonstrate that the New Economy is accessible along very different paths, underscoring the significance that different economic cultures have for competition, especially on the globalized world market. Given the diversity of markets on which the economy's future is decided, the concept that there are "varieties of capitalism" seems to describe reality more aptly than does the rigid demand for "standard capitalism."

Some readers may be surprised that this study takes them on a long tour of European economic history, though it is only a short side trip back to the Middle Ages and early modern times. That excursion appears unusual. After all, the idea is to grasp a phenomenon that, like the New Economy, still lies almost on the edge of the future. But it is necessary to gaze into this "distant mirror" in order to seek out the powerful institutions that make it possible from today's global perspective to demarcate paths of economic development, pat-

Notes for this section can be found on page 6.

terns of thought and behavior among collective actors, and the ground rules of economic life from one divergent economic culture to the next.

Not all institutions are so deeply rooted in history, however. The institutional framework still serving the German economy today emerged during the second German empire in the final quarter of the nineteenth century, about as long ago as the American structures, which also go back a hundred years. As argued in the present book, that period was the beginning of the German economy's entrance into the New Economy, whose hallmarks are market globalization and the primacy of scientific methods and theory in production processes. Of course, none of the organizational innovations distinguishing this new era draws directly on medieval or early modern models of commercial practice. Yet the German economy's propensity and capacity for integration of culturally endemic organizational principles such as autonomy, self-management, and the ability to cooperate into the practices of the new, postindustrial institutions can be understood only against the background of comparatively positive historical experience. This link is especially important because the New Industries, whose rise began before the turn of the previous century, operated on markets that handsomely rewarded precisely those social virtues. Hence, it is not enough to inform the reader of the causes, course, and impacts of the Second Economic Revolution in imperial Germany. In shaping this revolution, its two pioneers—Germany and the United States—relied heavily on their respective traditional arsenals of proven fundamental convictions.

Another major task of this study is to make out the essence of the German production regime. The German road into the economy of the twenty-first century is not a *Sonderweg*, not a special path. Its particular features and their many variations are characteristic of the path charted by numerous other countries. Most of what can be said of it pertains more or less to other European and Asian political economies, especially when they are seen in contrast to the American way of business, which seems to be on track to becoming the sole standard of best global economic practice. Using the United States as a benchmark is nothing new. The "American challenge" has been a common motif repeatedly igniting the imaginations of German and other European observers ever since the astute analyses by Alexis de Tocqueville and Friedrich List. More than a hundred years of transatlantic trade wars, economic penetration, and cultural competition have provided plenty of sparks for that process. The face-off between the American and German economic cultures today reflects an altogether ideal-type divergence.

Nevertheless, the starting positions of these two political economies in their race into the postindustrial age differ little. In the eighteenth and early nineteenth centuries, both countries were latecomers to industrialization. Almost simultaneously, they experienced modernism's breakthrough as the dominant order of business and society and ultimately set off for new shores along different routes in the late nineteenth century. In Germany and the

United States, the protagonists of the new epoch were the new industries, such as chemicals, machine manufacturing, automotive manufacturing, and electrical engineering. They all drew on science as a main factor of production, looked to the world market, and imposed revolutionary new rules on economic life. The principles underlying the success of the new industries have meanwhile permeated and shaped almost the entire economy in both countries, creating in each a "new economy" (hereafter *New Economy* when it refers to Germany), with a thrust of its own. These frameworks aim at quite diverse markets on which their respective institutional and material cost advantages can play out. The different requirements of the leading production methods in the two countries—diversified quality production in Germany and standardized mass production in the United States—therefore call for comparative analysis. Until the mid-1970s, it was mostly Fordism's triumphant global advance that posed the American challenge in the developmental phase of Germany's type of New Economy.

These matters notwithstanding, the striking thing throughout the twentieth century is the high endurance of the organizational principles and rules followed by the actors. The question about what gave rise to them thus also deserves keen attention in this study. Unlike the political development of Germany, the country's road into its New Economy was surprisingly straight and uninterrupted. The great political discontinuities of the twentieth century neither redirected nor appreciably obstructed it. From time to time, however, they did blur its contours to the point of unrecognizability and created special conditions of growth that fostered strategic mistakes in economic policy. Examples are the anachronisms that shaped economic development for long periods of the twentieth century in the wake of the two world wars and the attempts to cope with their legacy. To this day their consequences seem to complicate clear decision-making on the direction of economic policy. The most important thing that German policy currently needs is therefore a clear picture of the country's economic portfolio. What the economy can and cannot do is less a function of heroic decisions by policy-makers or the economic elites than of abiding organizational and market experience. That experience is the corporate, or economic, culture that delineates the latitudes for promising strategies in companies and economic policy.

The link between economic activity and culture is not self-evident. Nor is its nature illuminated by a diffuse concept of culture like that ushered in by the culturalist shift in the humanities—the human, or spiritual sciences. This link exists, however, and its intensity has tended to increase in the course of economic development. Economic activity and culture come from the same root. Without the human being's basic economic condition, that is, without the incentive to husband scarce resources, culture as the quintessence of the human race's emancipation from its natural state would be all but inconceivable. The very affinity between the concepts of culture and economic activity (including agriculture) supports this stance. Economics and technology quite obviously represent key spheres of culture, be it as discrete artefacts of homo faber or as settings that humans have created for living because nature itself does not provide them. The "mind as a form of organization" (Arnold Gehlen) that creates the institutional framework for continuity in human thinking and action and that thus guarantees societal life also suffuses the economy, which is ruled by its own laws. When resources are scarce, economic activity must always center on costs and possible alternatives for satisfying human needs. Whereas economists in modern times, as in traditional agrarian society, concentrated on the costs of the social exchange of matter (Karl Marx), attention in the twentieth century settled increasingly on the importance of comparative institutional cost advantages. Gaining them, however, requires social achievements that have "cultural roots" in a sense narrower than that of striving for material cost advantages in the social exchange of matter—which was the chief theme in David Ricardo's "law of comparative costs" and classical political economics in the early nineteenth century.

This narrower cultural prerequisite for acquiring comparative "nonmaterial" cost advantages includes the ability to create effective institutions that encourage a high degree of cooperation and, hence, a high level of trusting, cost-reducing cooperation in the economy.[1] Institutions as voluntary self-restrictions on personal freedom lead to thinking, action, conventions, "rules of the game," and informal and legal norms whose incentives and acceptance do not lie exclusively in economic advantages or constraints. They belong to that general act of interpreting and making sense of human existence and coexistence whose various manifestations differentiate long-standing "cultural groups" from each other. In this narrower understanding, culture creates not only "meaning" but also "utility" because stability and trust permit highly developed economic transactions at low cost.

Scholarly interest in ferreting out this connection flagged at times in the twentieth century. In the historical school of German political economics, study of economics from this cultural point of view was still taken for granted. Research therefore revolved around the question of the meaning and origin of institutions and the conditions governing change in them. When it was a matter of penetrating to the core of economic analysis, all that counted in the eyes of this school's most prominent figures was decipherment of the cultural code behind the economic facts. Mainstream thinking in economics a century ago still embraced the conviction that the state of the art does not advance by means of studies on the nature of commodities or capital but rather through inquiry into the causes of human difference and of the institutions that govern and influence the process of production and the distribution of goods.

If most economists nevertheless preferred to assume the prosaic nature of commodities and capital as the star of institutional economics rapidly set, it was because the institutional context in which economic activity could develop had remained relatively stable since the turn of the twentieth century. Further heed seemed unnecessary. This perception has changed dramatically since the 1990s. Institutional issues have recovered their place in university seminars, the management staffs of companies and associations, and government think tanks, bringing the cultural perspective of economic thinking right along. The expression "corporate culture" is perennially in danger of degenerating into a weasel word or, at best, of describing ephemeral and peripheral phenomena such as corporate design or corporate identity. As the following comparative analysis makes clear, however, corporate culture and economic culture have absolutely nothing in common with that interpretation. On the contrary, these two terms stand for the whole or the parts of the unmistakable institutional substance constituting the most important areas of the corporate and social system of production: corporate governance, the financial system, industrial relations, and so forth.

One reason for this renaissance of cultural factors in the calculus of current production functions lies in conflicts of the kind at the heart of the following study. The systematic character of this culture clash dictates against locating its main arenas in the world of daily politics. If Germany and the United States are once again redefining their mutual relationship, then it is the interests themselves that stand at the center of tactical and strategic policy considerations, not the cultural embedding of those interests, although it, too, is capable of eventually shaping national interests.

The present study of the escalating culture clash between different ways of acting and thinking in the world economy developed from my Pott lecture on Technology, Business, and Culture and draws on ingredients at very different stages of maturation. New ideas inspired by the question addressed by that lecture in Essen, Germany, stand side by side with arguments and facts that have already survived their scratch test in the academic community. Surprisingly, the state of historical research on the origins and development of the American production regime does not yet permit a complete comparison between the avenues of development taken by the two pioneers of the New Economy, the United States and Germany. The following study must therefore focus primarily on Germany's road, with the American development providing the background. The reader may judge whether the synthesis of my research has succeeded and whether the outline of the German path to the New Economy is suitable for answering a sufficient number of open questions. It goes without saying that a limited study, such as this one, cannot conclusively resolve the issues examined in the following book. Instead, the intention is to increase the degree to which they, and others, become integrated into economic history as a research paradigm.

This work owes its existence primarily to Jörn Rüsen. It was through his kind and gentle persistence that my manuscript for the Pott lecture turned into the book it now is. The Alfried Krupp von Bohlen and Halbach Foundation in

Essen enabled me to conduct research on the rise of the American production regime and continues to support that project. I am indebted to Matthias Band, Lars Heidemann, Petra-Monika Jander, J. Wesley Löwen, Christel Schwigon, and Frank Werner for their research assistance and technical help in producing the manuscript. I am very grateful to David Antal (Berlin) for his perceptive, faithful, and, above all, authoritative English translation of the German manuscript. The unwavering support of the publisher, Marion Berghahn, and the careful and professional work by the copyeditor, Catherine Kirby, and the production manager, Michael Dempsey, have been invaluable assets in shepherding the manuscript through to publication.

I sincerely thank every one of you.

Bielefeld, March 2005   W.A.

Notes

1   Francis Fukuyama, *Trust: The Social Virtues and the Creation of Prosperity* (New York: The Free Press, 1993), pp. 27–28.

I. A Living Past

1. Beyond "The End of History"

When the East Bloc imploded in the early 1990s, the American philosopher Francis Fukuyama spoke of the "end of history."[1] He meant, in Hegel's sense, the suspension of the great antagonism between the economic systems in East and West—between the First and Second Worlds—and, hence, the end of the idea of a dialectically mediated, progress-oriented synthesis of economic development bound to pull the Third World along gradually, too. The varieties of "Western" production regimes, for all their dissimilarities upon close inspection of their traditional institutional frameworks, counted little. As long as the East-West conflict also dominated the ideological struggle for worldwide political and economic hegemony, such differences were regarded only as facets of the same thing, the "free world's" market-based economic system. This monolithic perspective, a symptom of thinking in terms of blocs, quickly eclipsed the fact that World War II had also been fought as fratricide between differing branches of capitalism's extended family and that eliminating "corporatist" peculiarities of the German economic system had been a leading American war aim. It was the United States that therefore explicitly insisted after 1945 on trying German industrialists, whose heresy against the liberal creed of capitalism was partially blamed for the rise and crimes of the Nazi regime. Even before the end of the Nuremberg trials of industrialists, however, the wind of world politics changed and blew bloc-related internal disputes about the pure theory of capitalism into the background. The Cold War had begun, creating new, clearer-cut fronts in the competition for hegemony on the world's markets. All that mattered thereafter were economic efficiency and the ability to improve the economic stability and military defense of one's own camp as much as possible. Not until this East-West antagonism between the economic systems entered its final phase did it lose its capacity to mask internal divergence.

The face-off has recently yielded to a new economic worldview, that of global competition among numerous, institutionally different kinds of long-standing economic *cultures*. Speaking of "culture clash" in this context awakens associations with the "clash of civilizations" that Samuel Huntington considers to be the "central and most dangerous dimension of the emerging global politics."[2] But the conflict I mean is not one between groupings from different civilizations of world society. Nor is it about narrowing the view of the emerging world order to the monstrous and pathological, as insinuated in the rapidly swelling criticism of international globalization. The term "culture clash" is intended instead to characterize the competition that has broken out between the world economy's few paramount veteran economic and corporate cultures as they vie with each other over the rules of the market. The outcome of this contest for market hegemony will ultimately decide the extent to which economic cultures can hope to bring their respective comparative advantages to bear on the world market successfully.

The kid gloves have come off, certainly, but the competition does not usually overstep the bounds of civilized encounters. Although Vodafone's hostile takeover of Mannesmann AG and the takeover of Chrysler Corporation by Daimler-Benz AG, which for reasons of political correctness was announced as a merger, may be preoccupying the courts and inflaming the tempers of shareholders, the consequences of these battles are still manageable because of shared values extending beyond business as usual. The legal cultures, however, diverge as much as the economic systems do, making some decisions of American juries seem like statutory blackmail in European eyes. As shown by the reactions to Deutsche Bank's takeover of Bankers Trust Company and to Bertelsmann AG's challenge to the American media market, the style of contention becomes problematic when Germany's past is publicly instrumentalized to argue against German expansion on American markets.

Contradicting neoclassical economic theory, this competition for market success reflects the realization that there is more than one way to ensure long-term competitiveness on the world market. The path to achieving this objective need not be that of homogeneous entrepreneurial "best practice" incorporating the neoclassical ideal of deregulated markets and unrestricted entrepreneurial prerogatives. History shows that different market conditions can spawn different supply-side institutional variants. It also shows that a dense institutional landscape that has developed fixed rules, such as those in most European countries, is not necessarily less competitive than national economies with weak institutions, such as the United States, which leave organization and controllability primarily up to markets and hierarchies.

Essentially, the production regimes[3] of the leading actors on the world market in the early twenty-first century may be classified into two major models, each of which features institutional and organizational differences great enough to allow room for a number of its own empirical variants.[4] In English-speaking countries, the first model is known as a "coordinated market economy," or, with regard to its most important actor, a "business-coordinated market economy."[5] Its rules and the relationships between its actors fall within the purview of professional associations, such as the Federal Association of German Employers (*Bundesvereinigung der deutschen Arbeitgeberverbände,*

BDA), the German Trade Union Federation (*Deutscher Gewerkschaftsbund,* DGB) and its member unions, and the Federal Association of German Industry (*Bundesverband der deutschen Industrie,* BdI). It includes most continental European national economies, notably Germany, Switzerland, Austria, and Scandinavia, but also eastern Asian countries of Confucian tradition, such as Japan and South Korea.

The coordinated market economy is characterized by largely autonomous, self-governing economic players who interact in a spirit of cooperation and by an active role of government in which the state seldom goes beyond policies setting the overall context in which business is conducted. The government's input could, hence, be described as the production-related design, or "frameworking," of the social and economic system (*produktive Ordnungspolitik*). It is macroeconomic organizational policy. The state shapes the general organization and rules of the economy by influencing "data" through legislation, by shaping the infrastructure, by providing human capital within the educational system, and so forth. Employees and their unions are "incorporated" to a relatively wide degree into this system of balancing interests. The concept of macroeconomic organizational policy, of frameworking, contrasts with *regulatory* policy, which is understood to refer to relatively unsystematic interventions in daily processes and decisions. The more effective frameworking is, the less regulatory policy is needed.

The second model—the liberal market economy—exemplifies "uncoordinated" market orientation committed to the liberal principle of total competition. The relations between actors are not fully deregulated, nor is there a complete absence of institutions, especially since markets themselves consist of institutions and need regulation in order to keep functioning. The government has an active part in this regard, too, but *ideally* it plays this role mostly to guarantee the freedom of contracts and markets. By and large, the Anglo-Saxon countries are classified into this model. Since the late twentieth century, however, it has gained great worldwide appeal as well.

The measuring rod for the competitiveness of these regional, national, or global economic cultures is their ability to meet new challenges at any stage of economic development. Indisputably, these challenges are currently the growing worldwide interlinkage of markets and the increasing reliance on scientific methods and theory in the production process, phenomena for which observers have coined the expressions "globalization," "the communications revolution," and "the knowledge society."

Neither these pressing tasks nor the problems created by dealing with them are wholly new to the economic historian. The medieval economy had a well-functioning network of urban market relations spanning the entire known world before the advent of the territorial states.[6] The "capitalist world economy" of mercantilism harks back to the age of discovery.[7] Much more proximate are those processes and events whose roots lie in the past but whose effects are still very much a part of the present. Extending beyond the twentieth century, part of what ties this living past to the present is institutions that have determined the thinking and acting of economic actors for more than a hundred years; the other link consists of secular processes challenging the western economies in the early twenty-first century. Although they had already arisen in the late nineteenth century, they did not penetrate everyday awareness until just recently—globalization of the markets, and production's escalating reliance on science.

Historically speaking, the ubiquitous and palpable uneasiness about globalization is not new, either; nor is resistance to the growing dependence on anonymous markets and powers. Globalization reflects the intensifying interlinkage of world markets and connects people to developments over which they have little or no control. In particular, national and corporate autonomy in economic decisions is diminishing. The industrialized welfare state has always been at odds with its deepening integration into the world economy. But the huge, ever more dynamic economic potential that arose on the European periphery has seemed even more threatening from the start. It eventually cast doubt on the independence of the old continent. In the 1840s Friedrich List recognized that the United States would be throwing down the economic gauntlet of the future. To him, that confrontation (and the geopolitical threat that would emanate from the emerging "giant empires" of the United States and Russia) was the real problem. He sought to counter it with his political strategy for development and with a proposal for the formation of a Greater European economic area.[8] List was by no means the only person predicting this future. In 1835 Alexis de Tocqueville, who, like List, had firsthand knowledge of the United States, believed that the powers flanking Europe posed a long-term threat to the continent's economic and political autonomy. "Their starting-point is different, and their courses are not the same; yet each of them seems to be marked out by the will of Heaven to sway the destinies of half the globe."[9] However, confrontation over foreign trade policy did not occur with the United States until the late nineteenth century, when that country protected itself behind high tariffs and rode a wave of cost-reducing innovations in an effort to sell its burgeoning volume of mass-produced agricultural and consumer goods in Europe. From the European point of view, the history of globalization has always been closely linked to the American challenge.

The process by which production came to depend on science also began more than a century ago—around the same time as globalization. New sectors such as chemicals, machine manufacturing, and the electrical industry appeared, spawning a new paradigm of production: science as a production factor in a postindustrial economy marked by nonmaterial value creation. They were the germ cells of the New Economy, which has taken over their principles. Granted, the new vision long remained in the shadow of the industrial economy. Despite many setbacks, though, it unremittingly reduced material production's share of the social product and ensured that nonmaterial value creation steadily became the foundation of prosperity. An admittedly very simple, rough indicator may illustrate this role. The U.S. economy's real output measured in tons was about as great one hundred years ago as it is today. Its real economic value, however, has risen by a factor of twenty within the same period.[10] What has counted since then is the productive symbiosis between business and science. It brought forth its own institutions during the twentieth century and laid the cornerstone for a new social system of production clearly different from that of the Industrial Revolution of the late eighteenth century. The new economic base that coalesced at the end of the nineteenth century and developed into the economic standard for nearly all companies in the twentieth century ("New Industry") survived the ascendance of the American type of new economy just one hundred years later.

It is not so long ago that the historical social sciences focused attention on this development. In research on economic history, the new research paradigm was preceded by a sustained general attack on nearly all accepted facts about the Industrial Revolution.[11] By the end of this assault, the notion that the Industrial Revolution had been a radical departure from previous lines of development had been largely swept away. This epoch was no longer seen as a "take off" (W.W. Rostow). The century from 1750 to 1850 was interpreted instead as a largely continuous development of very long-term trends in the accumulation of human and material capital.[12] The concomitant historical mapping has profound effects. It raises questions about the significance of the Industrial Revolution as the economic departure point of today's economic and social conditions.[13] Given the gradual decline in the significance of material production, the neoinstitutionalist school inspired by Douglass C. North, who received the 1993 Nobel Prize in Economics, argues for seeing the end of the nineteenth century as the beginning of a new era in which the economic groundwork of the present age came together.[14] In his paradigm, the Second Economic Revolution, fundamental change in society's production potential stems from key changes in society's level of knowledge as well as from its ability to set up the institutional context necessary for drawing on this new dimension of production potential. According to this view, the revolutionary quality of economic development since the late nineteenth century lies not only in the close link between science and technology but also in the ability to mold institutional change into the organizational resources needed for mobilizing these productivity reserves on the markets, in companies (New Industries), and in the economy at large (the social system of production).

Contemporaries did not respond to these challenges uniformly by any means. Then, as now, most people hailed the scientific and technical revolution, although they were also quick to recognize and fear its impact as a "job killer." By contrast, dispute over globalization was stronger from the start. In Germany, the rise of new industries (most of which were export-oriented) and the powerful dynamics of the world market served to kindle heated controversy about the future of the nation's economy even before the beginning of the twentieth century, a debate that spread far beyond the academic forum and engulfed a broad segment of the public.[15] The fronts in this discussion pitted advocates of a semiautonomous industrialized agricultural state against adherents of an industrialized state dependent on exports. In essence, it was primarily about deciding on the viability of a strategy oriented to the world market, or, in today's terminology, the opportunities and dangers of globalization. It is true that anxieties about globalization and the ideological hardening of positions in the 1890s debate about the industrialized, export-dependent state had no measurable effects on the course of Germany's economy, which was oriented to the world market. However, their long-term consequences on the political mentality of the Germans and the mental mapping of German policy—before and after 1933—are unmistakable.

As World War II approached its end, the curtain opened on a new act of the same drama. The establishment of a new, open, multilateral world economic order was under negotiation between Harry Dexter White and John Maynard Keynes in Bretton Woods in 1944. Against the background of America's emerging hegemony on the world market, White, the closest associate of U.S. Secretary of the Treasury Henry Morgenthau, wanted to go far beyond creating a new monetary and financial system. He sought to pave the way for a global market economy that was intended to exclude Germany and give Great Britain a leading role.[16] Keynes, who made himself the spokesman of British and European interests, fought instead to preserve autonomous national scope of action in order to consolidate the most recent achievements of British wartime society: full-employment policy and its twin, the welfare state. Keynes lost this lopsided poker game but was vindicated by the development of the world economy from the early 1950s to the mid-1960s, those one and a half decades whose similarities in basic economic and social development have come to be known in Germany as "the long 1950s." In the summer of 1947, the imposed convertibility of the British pound sterling ended disastrously after only six weeks, suffocating for many years the hope for a rapid return to the financial freedom of movement that marked the period before World War I. It took a long time for the spirit of Bretton Woods and, with it, the American way of business to win out. The creation of the European Economic Community with its prospect of a large single market and the firming up of most European currencies in the late 1950s promoted the Bretton Woods world monetary and financial system and U.S. multinationals' penetration of the European market until the early 1970s, when the U.S. dollar was abandoned as the world's sole reserve currency. For many reasons, certainly one of them being the consequences of the Cold War, it was not until the 1980s that conflict broke out again between national regulation and globalization's "imperatives" of deregulation. Great Britain under Margaret

Thatcher was the first major European economic power to change course accordingly. In Germany the debate did not start until self-preoccupation with unification had lost its fascination and there was no more illusion that the "economic miracle" of the long 1950s could repeat itself across the country as a whole.[17]

2. The Splendor and Misery of Rhine Capitalism

Pressure on the German production regime continued to intensify as the American economy overcame stagnation in the mid-1990s and enjoyed a surprising boom while growth in the German economy, burdened by the costs of the country's unification, lagged behind that in other countries. With ever greater frequency, however, the widening gap in the development of the two world market leaders was also said to result from peculiarities of the German social system of production that liberal critics believed to be preventing the country from successfully tackling the challenges posed by globalized markets and the primacy of the scientific process in production. Germany's social system of production has since been the target of escalating criticism and has had to endure a painful examination of its "sustainability." Doubts have centered on the specifically German principles underlying the organization of the economy (production regime). Persistent mass unemployment since the late 1970s has led to more and more frequent claims that the German production regime is incapable of adapting to new, innovative product markets, for which globalization is said to require highly flexible entrepreneurial decision-making processes. Although faith in the economic and social "superiority of the Rhine model of capitalism" (Michel Albert) prevailed in the public discussion just ten years ago, and still does among many experts today,[18] mounting skepticism prompted speculation about the possible necessity of retreat, given the "political, media-related, and cultural influences of its American competitor."[19] The clash between American culture and Europe's leading culture, the German way of doing business, entered a new stage.

Until the 1990s the two systems were on a par with each other. In the twenty years before that point, the German, and then primarily the Japanese, production regime was even considered a beacon for the ailing American economy, whose decline was said to be arrestable only if it were to turn to the German model or "learn from Japan." Today, public criticism of the German model is aimed at precisely those elements that others prized in earlier decades: the long-term character of entrepreneurial decision-making and the

German production regime's close-knit cooperative structures, which make it difficult to adapt the system as a whole to new circumstances.[20]

Dissatisfaction with corporate governance is especially keen. It extends to the financial system, whose orientation to banks in general, particularly the all-purpose banks (*Universalbankensystem*), is blamed for the alleged undersupply of venture capital in the New Economy. There is also discontent with the system of industrial relations, whose German flagship—codetermination, or the right of workers to participate in shaping shop-floor conditions and management decisions—prevents quick decisions by senior management, and with the organization of businesses at the intercompany level, where excessive coordination by the associations leads to restraint of competition and overregulation of the labor market. Lastly, the dual system of vocational training is accused of compounding and perpetuating the entire situation through standardization of qualifications and through long-term mutual commitments between employer and employee.

Even where experts systematically consider the comparative institutional advantages of different production regimes (e.g., "varieties of capitalism") and not infrequently endorse the German version, the discussion usually lacks historical depth.[21] The shallowness begins with the analysis of the differences between the course of economic growth in the United States and that in Germany. Neither the causes of the American boom nor the reasons for Germany's weak growth are explicated.[22] Historical perspective is necessary, however, because it throws light on the existing capabilities of the economy's long-standing frameworks and organizational foundations. It is essential to an understanding of institutional processes of change because the present and the future are intimately linked to the past by institutional continuity.[23] The question about the origins of the German production regime is thus just as pressing as the issue about its change over time.

The most important facts about the continuity and change of the German economy's institutional framework (see Table 1) bring to mind astonishing things about the last century or so. As with the American social system of production, the German system with most of its components emerged more than a hundred years ago and has since defied all attempts to change it fundamentally. Opportunity to do just that arose after each of the two lost world wars and after the Great Depression (1929–1938), which was exceptionally severe in Germany until 1933. After 1945 the occupation powers took special pains to replace parts of the German production regime, such as all-purpose banks, the strong position of the trade associations, and the traditional kinds of cooperation between companies within their industries, with other, politically less tainted alternatives. These efforts led to discontinuities, which, in turn, were reversed with but few exceptions (cartels) with the consensus of German actors in the early 1950s, when economic efficiency regained priority over ideological needs in the United States, too. The German economy thereby managed to ward off most interventions. Turning to a social system of production that perpetuated patterns of the late nineteenth century, the country staged the economic miracle from the early 1950s through the mid-1960s. It goes almost without saying that this approach represented "continuity in change," which includes incremental changes of institutions that have kept developing along the originally chosen path. Changes of this kind can indeed be crucial in nature if they abide by the overriding principle of organization, as in the case of code-termination (the Labor-Management Relations Act),[24] competition regulations (antitrust law),[25] and provisions for old age (dynamization).[26]

Table 1. **Institutional Framework of the German Economy**

Social system of production	Production system	Legal system	Social Security system	Research landscape
Finance system: All-purpose banks (since the 1870s/1934/1952) *[1945–1952]*	Diversified quality production (since late 19th century)	Corporate governance: Joint-stock Corporation Act (since 1884/1897/ 1931/1937/1965)	Health insurance (since 1883)	University research (since 18th century/1819/1920/1969
Economic Interest Intermediation: Primacy of the economy (since 1879/1897); Primacy of the state *[since 1931/1933/1949]*	Growing share of nonmaterial value creation (in the 20th century)	Regulated competition (since 1897/1923/1958) *[1945–1951]*	Accident insurance (since 1884)	Unity of research and teaching (since 1810)
Intercompany system: "Corporatist coordination" (since 1879/1918/1934/**1936**/1949/1951) *[1945–1951]*	Dualism: Diversified quality production and standardized mass production *[1933/1941–1970s]*	Commercial law (since 1897)	Old-age insurance (since 1889/1911/ 1948/1957/1972/ 1992)	Applied research/technical colleges since end of 19th century/1949 Fraunhofer Society of Industrial Engineer-
Industrial relations: Codetermination (since 1890/1905/1916/1920/1951/ 1952/1976) *[1933–1947]*	Crisis in standardized mass production *[1970s]*	Civil law (since 1900)	Unemployment insurance (since 1927)	ing (since late 19th century)
Qualification system: Dual system of vocational training (since 1869/1897/1938/1969) *[1945–1951]*	Diversified quality production with mainly nonmaterial value creation (since the 1970s)	Welfare state: Socially equitable freedom of con- tract (since 1919/1949)	Long-term nursing care insurance (since 1995)	Cutting-edge research (Kaiser Wilhelm Society since 1911/1920/Max Planck Society since 1946/1948)

Note: Years in parentheses express continuity in change; years in italicized, boldfaced brackets express discontinuities.
Source: ©Werner Abelshauser.

With the "social market economy" erected after 1945, West Germany also had an economic policy compatible with the postwar social system of production. In practice, that policy—albeit not all of its conceptual utopias—has constituted part of the basic consensus of society in the Federal Republic of Germany regardless of changes in government coalitions. This coincidence and the repute of the economic miracle lent the old institutional framework of West Germany's economy a luster that enabled it to serve widely as a "model" at a time when even the normal dimensions of success to which it had receded since the mid-1960s still impressed most observers. Seen from this angle, the fundamental shift that has occurred in the relation between the models of cap-italism in Europe, Japan, and the United States since the 1990s is all the more surprising. The path of convergence seems preprogrammed; the pressure on Europeans and Japanese to adapt American "best practice" is rising. In short, the liberal model of the market economy seems to be establishing itself inex-orably as standard capitalism, with the coordinated market economy running the risk of slipping to the status of nonliberal capitalism, of being declassed as a deviant, perishable version of the market economy.[27] This situation confronts

German companies and economic policy with difficult decisions. It therefore seems worthwhile to become familiar with the origins of the German production regime in order to learn whether it really has become obsolete or whether one should not instead reform and retain a social system of production whose substance promises success even under current conditions.

Notes

1. Francis Fukuyama, *The End of History* (New York: The Free Press, 1992).
2. Samuel P. Huntington, *The Clash of Civilizations and the Remaking of World Order* (New York: Simon & Schuster, 1996), p. 13.
3. The term "production regime" emphasizes the way in which enterprises or sectors are organized. A close synonym used in this book is the expression "social system of production," which draws attention to the macroeconomic dimension. See J. Rogers Hollingsworth, "Continuity and changes in social systems of production: The cases of Japan, Germany, and the United States," in J. Rogers Hollingsworth and Robert Boyer (Eds.), *Contemporary Capitalism: The Embeddedness of Institutions* (Cambridge, England: Cambridge University Press, 1997), pp. 265–310.
4. See David Soskice, "Globalisierung und institutionelle Divergenz: Die USA und Deutschland im Vergleich," *Geschichte und Gesellschaft*, 25 (1999), 201–225; idem (1999), 'Divergent production regimes: Coordinated and uncoordinated market economies in the 1980s and 1990s', in Peter Lange, Herbert Kitchelt, Gary Marks, and John Stephens (eds.), *Continuity and Change in Contemporary Capitalism*, Cambridge, England: Cambridge University Press, pp. 101-134; Wolfgang Streeck, "Introduction," in Wolfgang Streeck and Kozo Yamamura (Eds.), *The Origins of Nonliberal Capitalism: Germany and Japan in Comparison* (Ithaca, NY: Cornell University Press, 2001), pp. 1–38.
5. The corresponding German term, *korporative Marktwirtschaft*, refers to an economy organized in such a way that neither the individual nor the state sets the tone. The rules by which it operates stem from a dense network of institutions and organizations whose actors in civil society (which Hegel referred to as "Korporationen") exist between the two poles.
6. Fritz Rörig, "Mittelalterliche Weltwirtschaft: Blüte und Ende einer Weltwirtschaftsperiode," in idem (Ed.), *Wirtschaftskräfte im Mittelalter: Abhandlungen zur Stadt- und Hansegeschichte*, 2nd ed. (Vienna: Böhlau, 1971), pp. 351–391.
7. Immanuel Wallerstein, *The Capitalist World-Economy* (Cambridge, England: Cambridge University Press, 1979).
8. Friedrich List, *Outlines of American Political Economy in Twelve Letters to Charles Ingersoll* (Wiesbaden: Böttiger, n.d.; original work published 1827); idem, "Über den Wert und die Bedingungen einer Allianz zwischen Großbritannien und Deutschland," in idem, *Schriften* (Berlin: Reimar Hobbing, 1931), vol. 7, pp. 267–296. (Original work published 1846)
9. Alexis de Tocqueville, *Democracy in America* (Trans. Henry Reeve), vol. 1 (New Rochelle, New York: Arlington House, 1966), p. 431. (Original work published 1835)
10. See Deutscher Bundestag, *Schlußbericht der Enquete-Kommission "Globalisierung der Weltwirtschaft—Herausforderungen und Antworten"* [Final report of the Inquiry Commission on "Globalization and the World Economy: Challenges and Answers"], Drucksache 14/9200 (12 June 2002), p. 260.

11. Rondo Cameron, "The Industrial Revolution: A misnomer," *The History Teacher*, 15 (1982), 377–384; idem, "A new view of European industrialization," *Economic History Review* (2nd Series), 38 (1985), 1–23; Nicholas F.R. Crafts, (1985), *British Economic Growth during the Industrial Revolution*, Oxford, England: Oxford University Press; see also N.F.R. Crafts and C.K. Harley (1992), "Output growth and the British industrial revolution: a restatement of the Crafts-Harley view," in *Economic History Review* (2nd Series), 45, 703-730; Jeffrey G. Williamson, "Why was British growth so slow during the industrial revolution?" *Journal of Economic History*, 44 (1984), 687–712; C. Knick Harley, "British industrialization before 1841: Evidence of slower growth during the industrial revolution," *Journal of Economic History*, 42 (1982), 287–289; Joel Mokyr (Ed.), *The British Industrial Revolution: An Economic Perspective* (Boulder, CO: Westview Press, 1993). On the preceding "silent revolution," see G. Hammersley, "The effect of the technical change in the British copper industry between the 16th and the 18th centuries," *Journal of European Economic History*, 20 (1991), 155–173; Roger Burt, "The transformation of non-ferrous metals industries in the 17th and 18th centuries," *Economic History Review*, 48 (1995), 23–45. On changes in industrial organization, see Maxine Berg, Pat Hudson, and Michael Sonenscher (Eds.), *Manufacture in Town and Country before the Factory* (Cambridge, England: Cambridge University Press, 1983).

12. Ester Boserup, *Population and Technological Change: A Study of Long-Term Trends* (Chicago: University of Chicago Press, 1981); Edward A. Wrigley, *Continuity, Chance, and Change: The Character of the Industrial Revolution in England* (Cambridge, England: Cambridge University Press, 1988).

13. Pioneers of this change in paradigm were Douglass C. North and Robert P. Thomas, *The Rise of the Western World: A New Economic History* (Cambridge, England, Cambridge University Press, 1973).

14. D.C. North, *Structure and Change in Economic History* (New York: W.W. Norton, 1981).

15. Kenneth D. Barkin, *The Controversy over German Industrialization, 1890–1902* (Chicago: University of Chicago Press, 1970).

16. See Wilfried Mausbach, *Zwischen Morgenthau und Marshall: Das wirtschaftspolitische Deutschlandkonzept der USA 1944–1947* (Düsseldorf: Droste, 1996) and Robert Skidelsky, *John Maynard Keynes: Fighting for Britain, 1937–1946* (Basingstoke: MacMillan, 2000), pp. 337–374.

17. Werner Abelshauser, "Aufschwung Ost: Erhards Illusion," *Die Zeit* (Hamburg), 19 March 1993, p. 36.

18. Steven Casper, "High technology governance and institutional adaptiveness: Do technology policies usefully promote commercial innovation within the German biotechnology industry?" (Wissenschaftszentrum Berlin für Sozialforschung, Discussion Paper FS I 99-307), Berlin, 1999; Richard Whitley and Peer Hull Kristensen (Eds.), *The Changing European Firm: Limits to Convergence* (London: Routledge, 1996); Hollingsworth and Boyer (Eds.), *Contemporary Capitalism*; Martin Rhodes and Bastiaan van Apeldoor, "Capitalism versus capitalism in western Europe," in Martin Rhodes, Paul Heywood, and Vincent Wright (Eds.), *Developments in West European Politics* (New York: St. Martin's Press, 1997), pp. 171–189; Richard Whitley, "Dominant forms of economic organization in market economies," *Organization Studies*, 15/2 (1994), 153–182; Louis W. Pauly and Simon Reich, "National structures and multinational corporate behavior: Enduring differences in the age of globalization," *International Organization*, 51/1 (1997), 1–30; Christel Lane, "Globalization and the German model of capitalism—Erosion or survival? (Discussion Paper, Faculty of Social and Political Science, University of Cambridge), Cambridge, England, 1999.

19. Michel Albert, *Capitalisme contre Capitalisme* (Paris: Edition du Seuil, 1991), p. 192.

20. Soskice, "Globalisierung," pp. 201–225.

21. See, for example, Peter A. Hall and David Soskice (Eds.), *Varieties of Capitalism: The Institutional Foundations of Comparative Advantage* (Oxford, England: Oxford University Press: 2001). See also notes 3, 4, 18, and 19 of this book.

22. On the issue in the United States, see Barry Bluestone and Bennett Harrison, *Growing Prosperity: The Battle for Growth with Equity in the 21st Century* (New York: The Century Foundation, 2000).
23. For the rationale underlying this line of thinking, see Douglass C. North, *Institutions, Institutional Change and Economic Performance* (Cambridge, England: Cambridge University Press, 1990), Foreword.
24. Werner Abelshauser, "Vom wirtschaftlichen Wert der Mitbestimmung: Neue Perspektiven ihrer Geschichte in Deutschland," in Wolfgang Streeck and Norbert Kluge (Eds.), *Mitbestimmung in Deutschland: Tradition und Effizienz, Expertenberichte für die Kommission Mitbestimmung* (Frankfurt am Main and New York: Campus, 1999), pp. 224–238.
25. Peter Hüttenberger, "Wirtschaftsordnung und Interessenpolitik in der Kartellgesetzgebung der Bundesrepublik," *Vierteljahrshefte für Zeitgeschichte*, 24 (1976), 287–307.
26. Werner Abelshauser, "Erhard oder Bismarck? Die Richtungsentscheidung der deutschen Sozialpolitik am Beispiel der Reform der Sozialversicherung in den Fünfziger Jahren," *Geschichte und Gesellschaft*, 22 (1996), 376–392.
27. Streeck and Yamamura, *Origins*, pp. 4–8.

II. The German Empire— Hothouse of Postindustrial Institutions

1. From Liberalism to the Coordinated Production Regime

The inception of the coordinated market economy as a new social system of production can be dated quite precisely. Beginning after 1873, it supplanted the old production regime in a process completed by the turn of the century at the latest. The replaced regime may be described as a "liberal market economy from above" and was the result of reforms designed to pave the way for the German states to enter modern times after the military confrontation with revolutionary France and the economic challenges of the English industrial revolution.

When the industrial revolution began in Britain, almost nothing of what was needed for a breakthrough to industrial society existed in Germany. Drawing conclusions from the French Revolution, some of the sizeable German states such as Prussia and Bavaria made it an early imperative of government policy to lay the foundations for modernization. The frequently quoted words of Prussian minister Karl Gustav von Struensee to the French ambassador in Berlin made this intention unequivocal: "The salutary revolution that you made from the bottom up will proceed slowly in Prussia from the top down."[1] Accordingly, the Prussian Civil Code (*Allgemeines Landrecht*) of 1794 released the peasants from hereditary bondage, albeit only on the royal domains at first. It pointed the way to a state ruled by law and under law, increasing the legal security of citizens and conferring property rights upon them. In short, it handed them the authority over their assets that the middle class in England had had to wring from the crown. This power of disposal is a basic prerequsite for the encouragement of private investment.

Despite these and other advances, however, reforms advanced too slowly, as soon became apparent in the clash with revolutionary France. The catastrophic defeat against Napoleon in 1806 fueled the doubts about the viability of a feudal society under a system of absolutist rule. But the debacle also forged the domestic political climate that made it possible to create in Prussia the conditions needed for radical, decisive state reforms under chancellors Karl Reichsfreiherr [Imperial Baron] vom Stein and Karl August Prince von Hardenberg from 1807 to 1820.

The emancipation of the peasants, which Stein's October Edict in 1807 declared for all Prussian lands beyond the royal domains as well and which was completed at midcentury, swept away the main obstacles to increased farming productivity. It thereby initiated the primary accumulation of capital in this stratum of society and helped mobilize new and free manpower for the industrial labor market of the future. Commercial reform, which introduced freedom of trade, among other things, strengthened the liberal bourgeoisie by fostering the economy's innovative forces. It created the context for large-scale forms of industrial activity, guaranteed businesses the free choice of location, and aided the mechanization of production. In 1807, of course, all these effects still lay in the future. By means of concessions and benefits, tax and fiscal reform cultivated entrepreneurial willingness to invest and, most important, widened the latitude for government financial intervention, which the state used to promote trade and industry. The formation of the German Zollverein, or Customs Union, in 1834 finally created a vast internal market, one of the most important steps in the development of market forces in Germany.

This "revolution from above" did not constitute an autonomous civil society, but it did bring about economic governance whose essentially liberal rules were guaranteed by the state. Royal absolutism changed into the rule of bureaucracy, whose power to intervene had to compensate for an absence of civil involvement. However, the economic success of this modernization strategy in German states was no less pronounced than that in other European countries. When business picked up throughout Europe in the mid-nineteenth century, Germany, too, had everything it needed for German industrialization and economic growth to take off.

Still not firmly rooted by 1873, confidence in this liberal order suffered a severe blow from the financial crash in May of that year (the *Gründerkrise*) and then eroded completely during the long, ensuing economic slump that terminated the prosperous early years of the second German empire. By the time the serious depression ended in the mid-1890s, the liberal order had given way to a new social system of production (see Figure 1). The shock waves that hastened the demise of the old system are familiar. So are the challenges that its successor had to deal with; the actors involved; the arenas in which the new patterns of action and organization were negotiated; and the thorny economic, social, and legal policy issues that tested the new rules of economic action. The "pattern of socialization" governing German commerce and industry, the context in which this birth process had to be embedded, is equally well known.

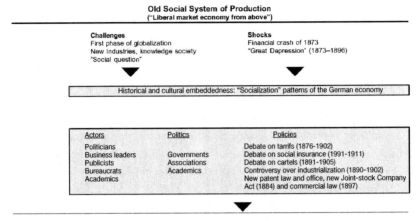

Figure 1. Hothouse of institutions.
Source: © Werner Abelshauser

And yet recent German economic history has few, if any, similarly significant processes whose essence has been so thoroughly misunderstood as this dramatic upheaval of the German production regime. In the tradition of debate about Germany's *Sonderweg*, the abandonment of liberal economic principles and the emergence of economic structures that initially seemed to correspond to traditional patterns have long been characterized as socioromantic and said to embrace a preindustrial value system. Some historians have gone so far as to see this retrospective orientation as one of the causes of the catastrophe that befell German politics in the twentieth century. By contrast, there is the fairly recent recognition that those departures gave rise to a new type of capitalism and civil society that stamped the German empire more with the hallmarks of the coming twentieth century than with the burden of the old order.[2] Going even further is the suggestion that "the staying power of the corporative interventionist state attests to its appropriateness and clout" and that "the development in the empire [must] definitely be considered modern and auspicious because it laid the foundation for the new real type: production-centered capitalism regulated by the interventionist state.[3] From this perspective Germany had to pay a high price in social and political instability for the fact that its economy marched in the avant-garde of the postindustrial era—and all that under uncomfortable conditions in terms of foreign policy and the world economy.

It is unclear, however, what this "modernity" and auspiciousness might consist in if not in a new role for the state. The first question from today's point of view is whether the production regime that originated in the empire and still prevails is prepared for tasks arising from the German economy's entry into the age of globalization and the knowledge society.[4] It is as disputable as ever whether the organizational and institutional manifestations of globalization's current dynamics have achieved an utterly new quality or, instead, whether they can be insightfully interpreted as part of twentieth-century continuity. Whereas sociologists such as James Rosenau[5] and David Harvey[6] diagnose in world society an "intensification" and "acceleration" of changes marking a sharp break with the past, economic historians such as Knut Borchardt and Richard H. Tilly warn against the "mistake of believing that the present process of globalization ... is to be regarded as something new and unique."[7]

Even before World War I, the key actors in a process of economic expansion that had transcended national frontiers included multinational enterprises, though not to the same extent or under the same conditions as today. Dating back in some cases to colonial times, the early transnational orientation and activity of Dutch, British, American, and German multinationals was a frequent topic of discussion[8] long before "globalization" became a household word in the late twentieth century. An additional corporative actor that contributed to the globalization of entrepreneurial activity primarily in the second half of the nineteenth century and the first decades of the twentieth has been identified as well: the free-standing companies, which, unlike the multinationals, operated only outside their home countries.[9]

The final third of the nineteenth century and the years before World War I were a high-water mark of global economic expansion in the macroeconomic sense as well.[10] Leading political economists of the German empire, such as the Berlin professor August Sartorius von Waltershausen, were convinced at the turn of the century that a new age was dawning in the world economy:

> The world economy ... is already so advanced that the drive toward a culminating form is visible in it. We do not know whether it will take hundreds or thousands of years to become a consummate social organism that systematically shapes its internal workings for purposes of optimal expediency, but we do have the right to believe that we find ourselves at the beginning of a development from which more is to be hoped.[11]

In 1914 foreign direct investment (i.e., without portfolio investments) amounted to no less than $45 billion.[12] This figure was the result of capital-market integration almost unhindered by capital controls. That level of integration was not achieved again until after 1980, when restrictions on capital movements in most Member States of the International Monetary Fund were finally lifted. Given the estimated annual international real net capital transfer of $0.4 quadrillion for the first half of the 1990s,[13] direct investment of $45 billion may appear slight. But with a U.S. GDP of $36 billion in 1914, of which foreign investment accounted for $7.1 billion (or 20 percent), the degree of capital interlinkage at that time was quite comparable to today's.[14]

The worldwide financial crash of 1873 showed contemporaries in Europe and the United States for the first time the extent to which capital markets had become interlaced in the capitalist world since the mid-nineteenth century. The collapse started in the United States and hit particularly hard in Germany, where many firms had just been founded in a wave that had already destabilized the economy. The crisis depressed investment returns for a long time, a period during which pressure grew for both countries to compensate the weakness of their own domestic markets by exporting commodities, services, and capital.

The interlinkage of the world market acquired a new dimension at the end of this major depression. Whereas the volume of world exports had risen by a quarter from 1872 through 1890, it *tripled* in the years from 1895 to World War I. The industrialized world simultaneously experienced a communications revolution every bit as significant as comparable processes today. In 1913, for example, the exchange of information between Wall Street and the London stock exchange took less than one minute. In the year preceding World War I, the number of multinationals and free-standing companies was probably no smaller than the number of enterprises operating transnationally now. The gold standard, which all important trading nations accepted, provided a global financial medium that has never been surpassed in its practical importance. The integration of the commodities markets and the networking of the financial markets achieved in this initial phase of globalization and then lost by 1945 in the catastrophes of the twentieth century's two world wars and the Great Depression were not fully regained until the end of the Cold War.

In summary, companies appeared as actors in a process of globalization in the late nineteenth century at the same time that the ascendance of the New Industries was heralding a shift toward nonmaterial, science-based value creation—a change that paved the way to the knowledge society. The long-term significance and impacts of this temporal connection has thus far not been studied. The intriguing aspect of the historical perspective is that the social system of production currently under renegotiation is the very one that emerged at this critical turning point of economic development.

This long-term temporal connection is the subject of inquiry in two ways in the following section. The first question concerns the historical and cultural embedding of the New Economy. What is the "pattern of socialization" on which the economy of imperial Germany was able to draw when it came to enriching newly created organizations with traditional institutional trust in order to keep their acceptance costs low? In the hothouse of institutions (see Figure 1), this "genetic constitution" was consciously used to refine the new drives (in both economic and ethical respects). The second topic is the new mode of economic interest intermediation—a current issue even today. The manner in which it developed in the political hothouse of the German empire between liberal and state-directed corporatism modeled the rise of the new institutional framework.

2. Patterns of Socialization Compared
The Economies of Germany and Great Britain

Germany—The First Postliberal Nation

The revival of the German economy that had propelled the industry of the empire to international renown in the final third of the nineteenth century is riddled with contradictions. After 1879 the empire reimposed protectionist measures on its foreign trade and payments even as it rose to become one of the most dynamic export nations in the world. The German states, which under the imperial constitution of 1871 retained the right to pursue their own domestic economic policies, returned to the principle of state interventionism in order to develop the productive resources of their "political economies." Until then they had used their power of intervention to dismantle vestiges of mercantilist economic structures and to orient the economy to the "reason" of the market.[15] Measures such as the nationalization of the Prussian railroads, their consolidation into the world's largest enterprise, and their use for opening up peripheral economic spaces; the planning and building of major canals; the introduction of interregional revenue equalization; and government funding of a new economic activity carried out by cities and local communities under the label of "municipal socialism" reminded contemporaries of Prussia's mercantilist era. Such leading economic researchers as Joseph A. Schumpeter therefore felt prompted to speak of the economic trends following the depression of 1873–1896 as the "neomercantilist" period.[16]

In a superficial sense, the German empire's economic policy interests also seemed regressive. Whereas the "decorporation" of civil society was pursued during the era of liberalism and public-law monopolies of the craft guilds and other market-controlling institutions were gradually eliminated, corporative principles began to reassert themselves in the 1870s and the years thereafter, albeit in new forms.[17] The 1890s, too—the years of storm and stress for German associations—had instances where people evoked "German history, especially that from 1350 to 1500," when they advocated the "cooperative state"

(*Genossenschaftsstaat*).[18] Attention was also drawn "to the economic importance of the old mercantilism" so as to emphasize "the necessity for a positive
state economic policy."[19] Even the cartel, that core institutional component of
new German industry, was regarded by contemporaries as "basically nothing
other than an application and modification of the idea of the cooperative association to modern industrial production."[20]

From Thorstein Veblen to Hans Rosenberg, critical analysts of German
social history saw a "deep gulf between the modern and traditional"[21] in these
conditions and developments. They found it to be a cause of tensions and
conflicts that seemed apt "to completely upset the balance of the social and
political, the spiritual and cultural life, the moral fabric and the religious foundations of a nation."[22] Bearing in mind the catastrophe of German history in the
first half of the twentieth century, Hans Rosenberg asserted that "lack of syn-
chronization between the different parts of the social system [threatened] the
system's viability."[23] But even without knowing what was to come, Thorstein
Veblen gloomily realized as early as 1915 that the empire—in his eyes "a bas-
tion of medieval thinking among the nations" and the very "embodiment of the
reaction against the emergence of modern civilization"—was "thus able neither
to decouple itself from the machine age nor allow itself to promote the industrial
economy for long, for it will eventually shatter the foundations of the state."[24]

The "German *Sonderweg*" paradigm, the critical variant of which under-
lies this formula, has long been resolutely challenged by Anglo-Saxon historians. Even the Bielefeld School, its erstwhile advocate, no longer defends it.[25]
The critics object primarily to the "primacy of preindustrial traditions" in the
explanatory repertoire of German historiography. They urge that one not only
trace the "feudal" continuities of German history but also account for the fact
that it was the society of German Emperor William II from which the most
dynamic form of European capitalism arose.[26] There has been much effort
since the early 1980s to put the "backwardness" of the political system into
international perspective and thereby acknowledge the peculiarities of German
history but dispute that its development was "unique." Did Germany complete
its civil revolution tacitly—whether "from above" or discretely through effective representation of economic interests—or did it disastrously fail to achieve
this goal? This question still frames the debate about a special German path.

Astonishingly little attention has been devoted to the methods of economic
and social policy and to the thinking and practices that, as institutional foundations, were closely linked to the success of the German economy. Did German
capitalism under the empire develop its dynamics because of, or rather despite,
the company social policy of its entrepreneurs,[27] the intervention of the welfare
state, or the market regulation exercised by the associations and cartels? Were
the collective bodies—the governmental, nongovernmental, and cooperative
organizational structures of the German economic order—"preindustrial"
anachronisms whose friction with economic reality was bound to thwart all

social progress sooner or later? Or can they be comprehended instead as precisely the bodies that incorporate appropriate ways of integrating economic behavior in response to the new kinds of challenges encountered in the age of advanced industrialized society? Lastly, what is the relationship between that newly emerged coordinated market economy and the preindustrial traditions so readily invoked by contemporaries in the German empire? If England can be called "the first industrial nation," is Germany then "the first postliberal nation"?

To answer these questions, one must ascertain the degree to which specific traditions of Germany's economic order abetted the shift in regulatory policy in the late nineteenth century. There are many signs that the contemporaries of Imperial Chancellor Otto von Bismarck and Germany's leading political economist, Gustav Schmoller, did not resort primarily to characteristic preindustrial features of economic behavior and thinking but rather to their outward manifestations in order to minimize the costs of hurriedly reorganizing the economy after the liberal era. The Germans took a different route into industrialized society, and their experiences along the way differed greatly from those of their neighbors. The merchant guilds and craft guilds and the mercantilist system exemplify this difference, as does a comparison between the conditions in Prussia and England.

The comparison with England comes to mind because key innovations in economic policy during the transition from advanced industrialization to a postindustrial economy appeared first in Germany, not in Great Britain, the leading industrialized country. New kinds of institutions—cartels, the welfare state, associations, the state's production-related design of the social and economic system—and the redefinition of interests in policy on the crafts and in the chambers of crafts, trade, and industry indicated that the German economy had finally caught up with England's development and was overtaking it. If these innovations lie in the developmental logic of a maturing industrial economy, as suggested by their subsequent imitation in other countries, why were they not produced first by Great Britain, the pioneer of industrialization? The answer to these questions is not only that the challenges and incentives of the markets in the two countries differed and thus encouraged correspondingly different approaches to the organization of their respective economies. It is also that the institutional innovations of the late nineteenth century are rooted in different historical experiences, which produced divergent patterns of institutional thought and behavior. The contemporaries of the German empire were well versed in corporatist maxims, which served as models in the process of institutionally refounding the social system of production.

From Autonomy to Self-Governance—The German Path to Industrial Development

As much as the craft guilds in England and those on the European continent resembled each other on the surface, they differed just as greatly in some of their pivotal functions from the very outset. The English craft guilds formed in the thirteenth and fourteenth centuries as the urban population underwent a social and economic regrouping brought about by an increasing specialization of commercial activity. The Gilda Mercatoria,[28] the merchant guild responsible for the trade monopoly that the king granted a city in return for its taxes, could no longer cope with these conditions. There is disagreement over the details of how the "mysteries" (from Latin *ministeria*, "occupations")—the "crafts" (*Gewerke*) and the "arts" (*Künste*), as the guilds are referred to in the sources—came to their privileges. Did the first craft guilds develop from serf artisans or from "foreigners," that is, from nonlocals or even immigrants? Did they achieve independence through agreement with the merchant guild or against the municipal authorities by way of royal charter? Evidence exists for all these possibilities.[29]

It is certain, however, that the English craft guilds did not acquire the same degree of independence as the German ones did. The English ones submitted to the existing state and municipal administration and accepted their view that the regulation of commerce was a matter for the state and its organs. Only in that capacity did the English craft guilds have the wish and ability to pursue their particular interests. England did not undergo a continental-style revolution of the guilds. The only craftsmen to lead a struggle against the patricians were those in London at the end of the thirteenth century, and the craftsmen lost.[30] Nor was the desire of the guilds to have their own jurisdiction ever as pressing in England as in Germany, for strong central authority kept the arbitrary administration of justice within limits. The cities seemingly weakened their authority by chartering the craft guilds with the crown's approval, but they actually strengthened their position by doing so. Tasks that were nothing but trouble for a central agency—questions of commercial policy, public security, and tax collection, for example—were delegated by the cities to the guilds, which the cities chartered but also controlled. The craft guilds thereby became vehicles for carrying out state and municipal economic policy. They remained subordinate to the city authorities. In 1410, York's knife-makers sought approval for their statutes by introducing their petition with the words, "To their very honorable and very reverend lords the mayor and aldermen of the city of York their poor fellow citizens address their supplication."[31] Such a subservient tone would not have been used by their self-assertive German counterparts. Whatever the reason was for writing down their charters, they could almost always invoke old customs and rights, as did Frankfurt's cloth makers in 1355: "We, the master cloth makers of Frankfurt, make known to our lords, the aldermen and the council alike, our customs and our due status, rights, and responsibilities, which we have long had."[32]

In Germany, too, the city dignitaries had originally reserved rights for themselves vis-à-vis the craft guilds. They demanded military services and taxes, appointed the guild wardens, and often deeply intervened in the commercial affairs of the guilds when it came to policies on food, police, and military matters. But most of these rights eventually passed to the craft guilds after bitter clashes, whether by revolution or, less dramatically, by purchase.[33] Although the craft guilds in Germany had also proceeded from free cooperative agreement, they were not really institutions under civil law. The German craft guilds had a rather public character, as the comparison with the English example illustrates. The German craft guild was a public office and agent of municipal economic policy, and in the absence of strong central authority it was of the greatest significance until well into modern times. The cooperative association of the artisans saw itself as an autonomous organization whose purpose was neither exclusively, nor even primarily, to pursue commercial objectives. It ordinarily also had general political, military, social, religious, moral, and legal goals. In the heyday of the guilds in Germany, commercial law started out as means to the ends of their cooperative structure, not vice versa, as was the case in England from the beginning. Precisely because the craft guild in England had not issued from an indigenous emancipation movement and partly because its use had been modeled on continental practice, it focused pragmatically on economic responsibilities, without developing its full political, military, social, religious, and legal meaning.

In the fourteenth century, compulsory guild membership became institutionalized in both countries. But whereas the Frankfurt cloth makers of 1355 were able to declare autonomously that "no one shall make cloth except our guild,"[34] the English craft guilds were subject to state intervention. In the Pepperer's Act of 1363, Edward III declared: "Item, it is ordained, That artificers, handicraft people, hold them every one to one mystery, which he will choose betwixt this and the said feast of Candlemas. And two of every craft shall be chosen to survey, that none use other craft than the same he hath chosen."[35] The craft guilds in both countries were thus of equal importance, but the foundations of their legal status and power were totally different. In London, however, the craft guilds prevailed politically as well: in 1376, the selection of the city administration was transferred to them, a right they finally confirmed in 1463 and exercised in amended form until 1835.[36] Practically every citizen henceforth had to belong to a craft guild. Even kings—from Richard II (1385) to Henry VIII (1484)—became honorary members of the "Taylors and Linen Armourers of the Fraternity of St. John the Baptist," one of twelve London guilds for gentlemen.[37]

The full development of the craft guilds was followed by their decline much earlier in England than in Germany. The importance of the active merchants and artisans gave way to the capitalists. Simultaneously, unbridgeable economic and social antagonisms opened up within the guilds. The concept that the craft guild looked after the welfare of its members and that these members constituted a fellowship for their common purposes disintegrated in the late fourteenth century. Nonprofit cooperative associations either dissolved into voluntary associations of gentlemen for filling community posts or became syndicates of small-scale capitalists. In one attempt to reform the craft guilds, the king and Parliament called a spade a spade in 1437 and sought to have justices of the peace and the highest municipal authorities tighten the supervision of the guilds:

> No such masters, wardens, nor people make nor use no ordinance which shall be to the disherison or diminution of the King's franchises or of other, nor against the common profit of the people nor none other ordinance of charge, if it be not first discussed and approved for good and reasonable, admitted by the justice of the peace, or the chief governors [of the cities and towns].[38]

At almost the same time the economic effectiveness of the craft guilds came under fire in Germany as well: "But if you want to be sure that things always go well and each person be true to the next, get rid of the guilds."[39] But this outburst was merely inconsequential complaining about profiteering. Until the 1700s the emperor and the territorial princes confined themselves mainly to taking action against "unreasonable practices" (*irrationabiles consuetudines*) of the artisans.

The guild system in England around 1700 comprised a wide variety of economic and social phenomena. There were the guilds of commercial craftsmen and small-scale retailers. As the "spirit" of capitalism and new production methods spread, mostly in the field of textiles, it diminished their role to the point of insignificance. The economic upswing circumvented the local industrial monopolies held by the cities of the old craft guilds. Instead, it tapped the reserves of energy and labor of the flatland or centered on cities such as Birmingham, Manchester, Leeds, and Halifax, "towns not wedded to ancient customs, franchises and liberties."[40] Under Queen Elizabeth I, the government tried to protect the guilds by introducing regulations such as the Statute of Artificers of 1563, which set the duration of apprenticeship at seven years and introduced the practice of regulating the level of wages in various trades. But none of the interventions during the Tudor period (1485–1603) withstood the pressure of the economic forces at work.[41] Nor did subsequent passing Stuart nostalgia for the solid "craftsmanship" of bygone days reverse, halt, or even slow the trend. But precisely because the old craft guild fossilized early, it was ignored by the rising tide of antimonopoly legislation. When freedom of trade was introduced in Great Britain in 1835 by the Municipal Corporations Act—even later than in Prussia (1811)—the legislation was purely a formality; the guilds had long since lost their monopolies on trade.

As of the fourteenth century, however, the guild system developed a different, more important, branch. New "bodies corporate" may have grown out of the old craft guilds by setting themselves apart through increasingly ornate guild uniforms or insignia, the livery of the successful merchant, or entrepreneur. They were therefore able to acquire new monopolies and become legal entities in their own right by royal incorporation. They embodied the commercial capital that won out in the fifteenth century. The cardinal criterion of these bodies was not one's origins or occupation, but one's property. Their relation to the crafts was that of a firm putting out work especially to people performing the work, at home (the cottage system, or domestic system). Their guiding principle was profit, not food. They supplied the crucial economic impetus in the transition to the mercantilist era. They had nothing in common with the old craft guilds except superficialities: the monopoly granted by the government, the commercial watchdog function that went with it, and the name. In reality, they embodied the opposite of what had once constituted the craft guild system, including the one in England.

The development of the German craft guilds took a different turn. Their demise was unmistakable, as was the weakening of the economic role played by the towns and cities with the rise of the territorial states. The crisis of the seventeenth century, specifically the economic stagnation of central Europe, intensified the distributional struggle between urban and rural areas, a conflict in which the craft guilds sought to hold their ground by enforcing a closed shop and preserving monopolization. The shift of the principal trade routes away from the Baltic Sea and southern Germany to Europe's northwest shrank the urban export industry in Central Europe and damaged the comparatively weak industrial base in the countryside. Given these economic realities, the guilds, in all their narrowness and rigidity, were not the worst obstacles to progress. On the contrary, restrictive commercial development compelled territorial economic policies to cling to the craft guild as an institution. The most widely read and highly regarded political economist of that day, Johann Joachim Becher, saw serious abuse in the guilds' certificates of apprenticeship, the membership restrictions based on the candidate's parentage, the ridiculously high standards that guilds came to set for the prescribed "masterpiece" by the aspiring journeyman (the proof of his technical competence), and the upholding of the honor of the trade, in short, their "malicious arbitrariness" and "secret monopoly." But he also argued that the immense freedom and competition, as it existed in England or Holland, held the artisans in constant poverty, with every work stoppage plunging them into terrible misery unknown in Germany. As he put it, only merchants and work outputters derived a proper advantage from it, and such a regime was possible only in a country with high export sales, such as the Netherlands or England. Becher concluded: "That is why the guilds cannot be dispensed with in Germany either, leaving every person to do what he wants."[42]

Abuse by craft guilds has been decried ever since they first formed. From the beginning, councils and sovereigns have occasionally responded by dissolving guilds and revoking their privileges. Such action did not translate into freedom of trade, however. It just meant that the guilds temporarily lost some of their political rights, wealth, tax privileges, and independent jurisdiction; that their wardens were turned into government councilors; and that the cooperative associations were made more dependent on the councils than they used to be. There was usually no change in the rest of the structure—the apprenticeship and journeyman system, the conditions of admission, the rights and privileges of the masters, the distinctions between one guild and the next, the regulation of competition by means of fees and strict product quality inspections by the guild or the town, the right to hold annual fairs, the laws by which foreigners and nonlocals were treated differently from nationals and local residents, the limitation on the number of members in a particular trade, not to mention the social and religious functions of the guilds. Even extensive reforms achieved conditions only equal to those in the heyday of the English craft guilds.

Among the craft guild reforms undertaken during the fifteenth and six-teenth centuries, those in Brandenburg were comparatively mild. Granted, after 1580 the guilds were required to obtain the Elector's affirmation of their statutes, and as early as 1541 the guild statutes "were approved with the pro-viso that it shall be possible at all times for the authorities to change, interpret, expand, or restrict the statutes as time may necessitate."[43] Nevertheless, the guild statutes were regarded as legitimately acquired rights whose confirma-tion was needed only as a formality and as a matter of fees. In principle, this arrangement had profound consequences because it turned free cooperatives into corporations chartered by the government. Nothing changed in practice, of course. In the promulgation of 1653 by Frederick William, the Elector of Brandenburg (1640–1688), the right of the craft guilds to exist was made con-tingent on the will of the state, but the Elector simultaneously assured them that the government was most determined to respect their age-old customs and traditions, especially in matters of discipline and integrity.[44]

A gradual shift began with Frederick William's death, which brought his son to power in 1688 as Elector Frederick III (later King Frederick I). The tran-sition necessitated the reaffirmation of the statutes, but the separate office, or "chancellery," handling feudal tenures was instructed not to tolerate craft guilds that continued to restrict the number of masters among their members.[45] At the dawn of the eighteenth century, Brandenburg's domestic policy was therefore seen in the Holy Roman Empire as relatively reformed and liberal. And it was the kingdom of Prussia, of which Brandenburg was a part, that showed the most zeal in bringing about the "Imperial Craft Guild Regulation" of 1731. Informed that the preferential position of the guilds had been exploited, the emperor proclaimed in Regensburg that his imperial majesty and the Reich were inclined to follow the example of other empires and totally dis-solve and eliminate all guilds so that the public would no longer have to suffer such outrageous private trade.[46]

The threat remained empty, though, particularly since the publication of the imperial decision, and therewith its ratification, took a long time in some territories, especially in the free imperial towns and cities. In Prussia, however, it appeared as early as 1732. Along with the general privileges granted by King Frederick William I, the craft guilds received standardized charters for the entire state in the period from 1734 to 1736.[47] These charters consolidated previous attempts at reforms in three ways:

1. The guilds were completely subjected to state authority.
2. Competition within the guilds was sharpened, and the structure of the local market was extended to encompass the territory.
3. The right of journeymen to ply their trade was reformed to guarantee their subordination to the police and the master craftsmen.

Once and for all, the craft guilds thereby lost the right to pursue their own economic interests and to control competition as they saw fit. The old forms of vocational education and the organization of guilds as cooperative associations endured for the time being, however, ensuring a functional system of job placement and securing commercial and occupational support. The social importance of this point is great. In 1800, for instance, the Duchy of Magdeburg still had 7,000 to 8,000 people working in cottage industries, the factory system, mines, and saltworks—with much of that labor force operating in guild-like structures—as opposed to 12,000 to 14,000 artisans.[48] According to a survey taken in 1861, factory workers outnumbered artisans (56:46 percent) only in Saxony, whereas in Old Prussia artisans (59 percent) clearly constituted the majority of persons classified as "skilled workers" or "artisans"— about the same relation as that for the Zollverein overall in that year.[49] In Prussia, the craft guilds did not retard industrial progress. The system's economic and social survival and its formative power over industrial institutions and vested interests until well into the twentieth century owed at least as much to the reforms as to Prussia's relative backwardness.[50]

Unlike the craft guilds in England, which had withered in the shadow of capitalist development by the seventeenth century, those in Prussia, as in the other German territories, had a different future. Although their legal form was cut back, their social impact remained unchanged until the economy's complete industrialization, and long thereafter in many cases. Criticism of the craft guilds centered on their abuses, but it left their values and principles untouched. In the public mind, the cooperative contract and the primacy of common interests morally outranked buying, founding, stock trading, and speculating.

Market and State—No Antagonism

The issue of monopolies and the role of government is yet another area where comparison between England and Prussia, including other German states, reveals the characteristic difference that so decisively affected the path of the German economy. It is not solely about the leads and lags of industrialization. The battle cry of Cromwell's period, "freedom, property and trade," launched a continuous movement toward individualization in England before the age of state mercantilist economic policy had actually ever begun in Prussia. Yet under the Stuarts, too, whose economic policies featured protectionism abroad and royally sanctioned private monopolies at home, the experience of the English differed greatly from that of the Prussians in their mercantilist period.

Under Elizabeth I, the monopolistic organization of early capitalist industry experienced its first boom, with monopolies accounting for nearly every article.[51] However, the death of the queen in 1603 meant the end of unchallenged royal rule, the basis of the right to bestow exclusive authority to run a particular business. Thereafter, the crown's prerogative to authorize monopolies became the main bone of contention with the aspiring middle class. From time to time, Parliament had already been up in arms against the deleterious effects of "charters and letters patent of divers kings" (1504).

Parliament wished to recognize only the protection of inventors, which usually lasted fourteen years, and the local monopolies that incorporated guilds held "in the common interest." The Statute of Monopolies of 1624 therefore stated:

> That all monopolies, and all commissions, grants, licences, charters and letters patent heretofore made or granted, or hereafter to be made or granted, to any person or persons, bodies politick or corporate whatsoever, of or for the sole purpose of buying, selling, making, working or using of any thing within the realm ... are altogether contrary to the laws of this realm, and so are and shall be utterly void and of none effect, and in no wise to be put in use or execution.[52]

The House of Commons regarded the monopolies as the main cause of rising prices and deteriorating quality, and it questioned their commercial utility. The lines of a tedious debate over principles were drawn. The corporative and monopolistic mercantilism of the Stuarts used the granting of monopoly rights and patents primarily to open up fiscal sources not subject to the control of the Commons, but it defended the practice on the grounds of development policy. On principle, therefore, King James I advocated a ban on monopolies but did not want to forfeit the economic (and fiscal) blessings of government support for industry. The Statute of Monopolies, with its numerous exceptions, offered a good basis for balancing the two aims. The statute's patent clause, which provided fourteen years of protection, and the prerogatives of the guilds were the primary tools for legitimating monopolistic privileges. One of the most unpopular of them was the soap monopoly granted by James I in 1622 and confirmed in 1631. It survived for several decades, giving Sir John Colepeper ammunition in 1640 for his convincing stance as the champion of the entire empire when he decried such privileges before the House of Commons, sarcastically inveighing against "monopolers and polers of the people":

> These like the frogs of Egypt, have got possession of our dwellings, and we have scarce a room free of them; they sip in our cup, they dip in our dish, they sit by our fire; we find them in the dye-vat, wash bowl, and powdering-tub; they share with the butler in his box, they have marked and sealed us from head to foot.[53]

In reality, the attempts to nurture new industries and expand old ones by chartering monopolies usually failed. One of many examples is the dyed-cloth monopoly granted in 1615 by James I, who flanked it with an export ban on white fabrics. The hope of establishing this industry in England was dashed just two years later by sluggish sales for both kinds of cloth because the one did not prove good enough for export and the other had meanwhile lost its place on foreign markets. The project not only ended with the bankruptcy of the chartered company owned by Alderman William Cockayne, it also dealt a severe blow to the entire English textile industry. James I, too, finally had to admit that the project had miscarried.[54] This realization, however, did not keep his successor, King Charles I, from exempting numerous companies from the ban on monopolies. He issued royal charters bypassing Parliament in order to create sources of income for himself. Not until the Bill of Rights, passed in 1689, as a result of the Glorious Revolution, did Parliament eliminate the royal right of dispensation together with the royal regalia for mining.

The double stigma of economic ineffectiveness and political arbitrariness did not fully prevent the formation and survival of cartels in the eighteenth and nineteenth centuries. The most important of these organizations was probably the Limitation of Vend, the association of owners of Newcastle collieries. It existed from 1771 until 1844 to ensure the stability of the London coal market, which was supplied by sea from the pits in the counties of Durham and Northumberland.[55] Unlike the circumstances in Germany, however, strict court rulings and public hostility toward monopolies limited the effectiveness of monopolistic market structures to such exceptional cases and short-term cyclical emergencies.

The government official as a social figure, the state interventionism of the Tudor and Stuart periods, and the monopolies all became caught in the disputes between the crown and the middle class. The ambitious notions that the early Stuarts entertained about the role of the English crown in Europe far outstripped the king's possibilities of financing them from his own wealth and tax sources. Sales of crown lands soon reached their limit because they depressed land prices to a level that diverted more savings into farming—much to the detriment of industry—than would have been the case without state intervention. The tax burden at the beginning of Stuart reign was rather modest, particularly in comparison to that on the continent. As stressed by John Aylmer, a contemporary British pamphleteer referring to German conditions in 1559:

[The Germans] paye till their bones rattle in their skin: and thou layest up for thy sonne and heir. Thou are twise and thrise in thy lifetime called uppon to healpe thy Countrye with a subsidie or contribution: and they daily pay and never cease. Thou livest like a Lorde, and they like dogges.[56]

The British taxpayers reacted all the more sensitively to attempts of Charles I to open up new tax sources by going around Parliament and thus violating their property rights, although these actions were defended by the highest court in the land as "emergency measures." Such was the case with the "ship money" collected for the first time in 1634 and repeatedly thereafter, ostensibly for combatting piracy. Lack of money was also what finally helped local administration, through the justices of the peace, prevail over the civil service. The justices of the peace usually came from the local gentry and were able to forgo the pay to which they were entitled.

The intention of Charles I to create a state bureaucracy with the assistance of the Church of England did not fail solely, or even primarily, because of the crown's precarious financial circumstances. The vision of having the state regulate industry and foreign trade through a system run by guild officials rather than capitalist trading companies, of channeling investment into preserving and creating jobs, and of caring for the poor in order to maintain peace and order addressed the need for stability during that crisis-ridden time.[57] Moreover, the civil war rent the emerging capitalist class in two, making it difficult to reduce the conflict to antagonism between new and old principles in the economy. It is equally doubtful that economic causes played an overriding role in this dispute.[58] Be that as it may, nearly every economic policy measure of the Stuarts deepened the split in English society. The plan to create national guilds may have given advantages to the artisans and merchants organized in guild-based industry and may have helped stabilize the domestic market in the crises of the early 1720s and 1730s. But it violated the interests of those for whom running a business without outside interference from the rigid rules of the guilds had long come to be seen as their due. The preferential status accorded major foreign-trade companies accommodated the wishes of individual groups of capitalists but inevitably infringed on the interests of others. The effort to improve the quality of English brands eventually strengthened Britain's position on the world market and met basic standards of justice and fairness, but in the economic crisis of the seventeenth century it temporarily impeded flexible adaptation to the market and exacerbated unemployment.

The crown's overthrow in the civil war also meant the defeat of state interventionism. Its institutional foundations—the absolutist councils and chambers, such as the Star Chamber, the Council in the North, the Court of Wards and Liveries, and the High Commission—vanished forever. For the civil servant in England, the reversal resulted in social disdain, inferior status in higher society, and discrimination in favor of the industrialist, merchant, or landowner.

This fate is another historically powerful difference between the experience in England and that in Germany.

There was little friction between the cameralism of the German territories, specifically Prussia, and a middle class not yet greatly inspired by the capitalist "spirit" ("Accumulate, accumulate, that is Moses and the prophets!"[59]). Government control over economic policy was perpetuated by the marked antipathy toward individualism, which threatened class boundaries and clothing regulations. On the whole, the Lutheran concept of economics clung to medieval economic ethics, which saw "something really divine" in the state.[60] In most German territories, enlightened absolutism earned the respect of "the middle class" by pursuing a domestic development policy supported by a comparatively efficient system of civil servants. From the mid-seventeenth century on, the power of the estates steadily waned, and officialdom was in the ascendance. The Elector of Brandenburg, determined to unite his state after the Thirty Years' War, recruited a "privy council" from all his provinces, often reinforcing it with "foreigners," to pave the road for economic reconstruction and development "from above" for lack of private initiative and middle-class economic power. In the reign of King Frederick William I (1713–1740), district councilors and tax commissioners represented the very incarnation of the well-meaning paternalism of the enlightened despotic police state, which initially used its powers of intervention primarily to fight corruption and local nepotism. If the Hohenstaufen dynasty (1138–1208 and 1215–1254) created the first real class of officials for the ministerial organization of the Holy Roman Empire and thereby paved the way for the realm's economic prosperity, such influential nineteenth-century political scientists as Gustav Schmoller viewed Prussia's administrative reform as a further indispensable step toward lifting the state above the level of "tendentious class rule": "The propertied classes calmly nestled into town and countryside, plundering state power more and more to enrich themselves, until the Prussian monarchy and enlightened despotism finally brought change with their officials."[61] Given this analysis, it is no wonder that Schmoller considered the state to be "the most magnificent moral institute for the education of the human race" and wanted to invest it with "narrower or broader [responsibilities], depending on the cultural conditions."[62]

The step of bringing the administration of justice under government control in the second half of the eighteenth century during the reign of Prussian King Frederick II (1740–1786) completed the creation of a state bureaucracy. Up to then, the justice system had lain mostly in the hands of untrained privileged individuals of the upper class who used their positions as sources of income and power. Frederick II placed the courts in the care of professional judges and lawyers and in 1748 relinquished royal fiat that intervened in the course of civil justice, a renunciation that Frederick's successor codified in the Prussian Civil Code of 1794 (though exceptions did occur in penal matters). These state reforms of the justice system, as with the economic reforms of the early nineteenth century, gave the capitalist forces legal security and that essential element for the rational functioning of a private economy—property rights. Although Carl Gottlieb Svarez and his coauthors of the code did not manage to win the conservative opposition for all their ideas, the outcome came close to the objectives that Svarez regarded as the ideals of Prussian governance in his addresses to the crown prince:

> Absolute regularity throughout government administration; strict supervision of prompt and unbiased administration of justice; constant alertness that one strata or class of the nation does not curb the rights of others [and] that the poorer and more subordinate man is not oppressed by his wealthy and more powerful fellow citizen; unflagging care to the creation and support of public-welfare institutions, through which the prosperity of the individual can be enhanced [and] through which farming, manufacturing, and factories can be promoted; respect for civic liberty, for the rights and property of the subjects; and, finally, complete freedom of religion and conscience—these are the basic pillars of the system of Prussian state governance.[63]

The paternalistic and bureaucratic regime of absolute sovereigns in Germany took the role of the "good policeman" and acted in the interest of the common weal more than was the case in England at a like stage. It also developed an outstanding bureaucracy that lasted longer than the arrangement under the Stuarts. Both of these facts explain why the German middle classes remained sympathetic toward state interventions and bureaucratic administration even when the disadvantages of state tutelage became perceptible despite its positive intentions. In fact, the figure of the "private official" transferred the principle of bureaucracy seamlessly into the sphere of the capitalist economy.

Vastly different preindustrial traditions of England and Germany show through in yet another way, too. The bureaucratic, interventionist state in England threatened the self-won property rights of the middle class and, hence, the keystone of the institutional change that had ushered in economic growth, whereas the state in Germany first established the rights of disposition over productive wealth and anchored them in due process.

In retrospect, the shift to a new production regime based on a coordinated market economy and (neo)corporatist interest intermediation through components of a welfare state, market regulation, and intervention has its roots in the interaction of three factors. First, Germany, the belated industrial nation, had to face up to the change in the economic and social structures of the late nineteenth century if it wanted to overtake the leading industrialized powers without being able to make up the lead they had in every respect. The challenge of economic backwardness is thus what led to Germany's development of effective institutions in many areas.[64]

Second, backwardness as measured against the state of England's middle-class society was not exclusively a challenge for Germany on its path to industrialization. Paradoxically, backwardness also facilitated the necessary adaptation to the change in economic and social structures of the late nineteenth century. The Prussian state had pressed the industrial revolution "from above" since the Stein-Hardenberg reforms, without identifying itself with the interests that the industrial middle class had in acquisition. Bureaucracy and feudal agrarian anachronisms of power did not prevent industrialization in Prussia and other German states but, unlike the case in England, did keep the state cool to a specifically liberal brand of capitalism focused on enrichment through the market. The priority of the political leadership and the senior bureaucracy on putting the stability and security of the state above the rational profit drive of particular groups in society made it easier than in England to ignore short-term negative impacts that the new course had on private interest in acquisition.

Third, this process of adaptation was also promoted by traditional regulatory habits of thought and experience that remained virulent into the nineteenth century in Germany and that seemed in principle to be in keeping again with the new conditions. Only epigones of early nineteenth-century romanticism in political science succumbed to the temptation "to put new wine into old bottles." They wished to resurrect forms of the medieval corporation for late nineteenth-century economic and social needs because those structures had supposedly "created and sustained prosperity [and] had guaranteed and protected freedom."[65] There was, however, growing willingness "to revisit those facets of civil society between the individual and the state that, through the higher power of a large community, unite the knowledge about the needs of compatriots with the interest in satisfying them" so as to overcome the "rigid dualism" between the "atomism" of isolated individuals and the "oppressive, mechanical, busybody rule of the state.[66] Given the "recency of complicated economic conditions," German political economists were also more willing than their British colleagues to abandon the notion that "progress from coercion to freedom could ... be a simple ascending curve." The German observers favored a cyclical model of order that posited changing technical and economic constellations and that did not dismiss the experiences of earlier eras as completely obsolete.[67]

There were only a few cases in which this preference led directly back to old institutions such as the guilds, which were reactivated in the shrinking old middle class. More typical was the rise of new institutions and forms of organization—the modern welfare state, trusts, and state interventionism in economic policy, for example. They were consistent with new needs because they owed their emergence to a growing concentration of capital; marked cyclical fluctuations of prices, returns, and production figures; rising demand for mobility on the labor market; and the overall increase in the complexity of conditions for stability in industrial society. These new institutions and forms of organization also met the needs of the postindustrial era, whose most important manifestations were market globalization and the ever greater role of science in production processes. Links to the economic conditions of the early modern period were very abstract at best, and even less clear for the Middle Ages. Yet those widespread, deeply rooted, and, for the most part, positively associated historical experiences helped the institutional innovations of the postindustrial economy make an early breakthrough in the German empire (see Figure 1). By contrast, the same economic tasks in the United States elicited institutional solutions that corresponded to British experience and that remained part of the middle-class, liberal heritage of the American colonies after the War of Independence.

3. Interest Intermediation between Societal and State Corporatism

The Century of Corporatism

The "century of corporatism"[68] seemed to come to an end prematurely and irrevocably in 1945. The corporative idea, contaminated and discredited by the fascist regimes in central and southern Europe and by German National Socialism, was indisputably one of the casualties of World War II. In the altered economic and social conditions after the war, even liberal variants of corporatist interest intermediation, such as Roosevelt's New Deal,[69] gave way to the return of freer game plans in economic and social policy. Particularly in West Germany and Italy, which both had rich, albeit ultimately painful, experience with the corporatist way of articulating interests, thirty years of extraordinarily successful economic development and great social stability had driven the corporatist tradition almost completely from the public mind.

This outcome was bound to have an impact on historical research. Even as late as the present discourse about the "sustainability" of the German economy, the amazing late nineteenth-century metamorphosis that turned a backward Germany into Europe's most advanced economic nation is commonly measured with the yardstick of Anglo-Saxon-style democracy and liberal ideas about representing and communicating interests. From this point of view, Germany must indeed seem to have been following a "special path," for although the country developed a sophisticated system of trade associations and pluralistic interest intermediation, parliamentary democracy and its institutions failed in Germany to acquire the political importance and social acceptance marking comparable industrialized societies of that era. In addition, many of the "new" elements of the institutional framework, such as corporations, trusts, and councils, seemed to have sprung more from the preindustrial order than from the spirit of capitalism characterizing the period of advanced industrialization. Does it not stand to reason that the inherent problems of German society, of which there were none too few, are attributable to this asymmetry in economic and social structure rather than to unusually rapid structural change and economic growth? Was not the debacle of the Weimar Republic due not only to foreign policy burdens but also to the weakness of its liberal democratic traditions, whose most obvious manifestation was the inability of the Reichstag, the lower house of parliament, to stand its ground against powerful interest groups? In many respects the history of the German empire and the Weimar Republic was certainly no success story. For that reason, institutions and political behaviors to which the German business community gave rise did not initially seem to merit examination for innovative contributions and for the degree to which they served as models for that segment of European economic developmental processes.

This view shifted only gradually, and not before the mid-1960s. Without explicitly touching upon the historical dimension, Andrew Shonfield's brilliant analysis of modern capitalism[70] as *geplanter Kapitalismus*[71] (planned capitalism) showed that planning, not competition, and that corporative (no longer meant pejoratively), not pluralistic, rules informed the postindustrial economy at precisely the points where it operated with the greatest success. The focus on the functioning of the *present-day* political system of the developed capitalist countries was even greater in the nearly twenty-year discussion about "neocorporatism" that Philippe C. Schmitter triggered in 1974 by asking whether it is "still the century of corporatism?"[72]

Schmitter posed this question because he recognized that the process of empowerment on both economic and political "markets" was so advanced that the fiction of free competition and freedom of contract was no longer credible in light of inequality in the distribution of power and material resources. By eliminating the pretense of equality between social groups in the process of communicating interests, the concept of corporatism opened the way for research on urgent problems.

Two issues were central: the critical interest in uncovering social power structures, and the explanation and improvement of the conditions for stability in economically advanced democracies. The debate on neocorporatism was also based, usually implicitly, on traditions in the history of human thought and institutions that were widespread in central Europe up to at least 1945 and, in less explicit forms, continuously beyond that point.[73] German experience with organizing ways to balance economic interests during the empire and the Weimar Republic thus resurfaced as a focus of attention. This time, however, the era was no longer treated more or less exclusively as a study in the collapse of a leading postindustrial nation and the failure of German democracy. It was examined instead primarily as the historic starting point of current trends in postindustrial interest intermediation, which have tended to draw reproach again since the 1990s.[74]

In the corporatist model, the balancing of interests is not seen as a market process whose ability to function derives from the principle of competition. Rather, it is characterized as a political cartel of the "major" social groups, which cooperate closely in dividing the "market" among themselves. This practice requires a high degree of autonomy and self-governance from the participating trade associations and unions, which are simultaneously involved in national economic and sociopolitical decision-making. By distinguishing between liberal (or societal) corporatism and authoritarian (or state) corporatism, Schmitter made the approach acceptable again for analyzing interest intermediation in democratic societies and freed the "German model," which had enjoyed wide international respect in the 1970s, from its contamination with authoritarian facets of German history. His distinction cast state corporatism as a frequent symptom of the antiliberal, authoritarian state that lags in economic development. Societal corporatism, by contrast, became an important, perhaps even essential, part of the postliberal, late-capitalist democratic welfare state.[75] The two variants differ on the role of the state, depending on whether the process of balancing interests results from general economic and social developments and voluntary agreements or from governmental requirements. Another important point is whether state control stems from mutual agreement or from coercion. Both types figure in the development of German interest intermediation in the twentieth century.[76]

This train of thought raises the same questions as those posed about the emergence of collective regulatory and decision-making structures (i.e., those set up by associations and cooperatives) against the background of the German economy's specific conditions of socialization. Does neocorporatist interest intermediation lie in the tradition of preindustrial structures? Or does it not instead embody forms of the sociation of economic activity that, in the age of the Second Economic Revolution, are understandable as a suitable response to internal and external challenges confronting the German economy since the late nineteenth century? Did the triumph of industrialization in Germany manage to produce a liberal society and democratic institutions that would have given the necessary political stability to rapid economic structural change? Was Germany able to become the first postliberal nation in Europe and take the lead in the process of social development, as it did in the realm of economic growth, the change of economic structure, and the formation of a postindustrial production regime? Did the Weimar Republic's policy of balancing interests come to nothing *despite* rather than because of its basic corporatist pattern, which was a more advanced approach to interest intermediation than other countries had?

The Failure of State Corporatism in the German Empire

Rocked by the financial crash in May 1873 and the onset of the severe depression that followed, governments in the young German empire's constituent states, specifically Prussia, reclaimed old responsibilities and seized others.

During the 1870s, overall awareness of the social character inherent in the economic processes of production, distribution, and consumption increased. For that reason, state intervention responded to the pressure of the crisis by changing both focus and character. Most innovations, and by far the most important ones, came in the economic policies of Germany's individual states—production-related state frameworking of the overall economic and social system and sectorial support of the economy, for example. Though enacted because of the desire of certain groups to hold onto power, these changes proved to be trendsetting and historically durable "postmodern" elements of German economic policy.[77] It was there, not in foreign trade, that the decisive shift in the regulatory policy of the German empire took place. It included the attempt to restructure the economic order of the empire, starting with Prussia, in the direction of a corporatist system.

The first points of departure for this effort lay in the new economic policy oriented to the internal development of the Prussian state. Initiatives of this kind did not come only from the ministries; the ministries created advisory bodies that brought together representatives from industry, agriculture, and public life. These committees were set up at the district level (e.g., railroad councils and a provincial waterways board) and at the *Land* (state) level (e.g., a state railroad council and a state waterways advisory board). Superordinate economic policy issues crucial to the planning of private industry were subject to a constant process of public deliberation and balancing of interests. State intervention in the economy was thereby linked with the interests of important groups in society, which were simultaneously incorporated into the framework of government economic policy. Another aspect of this development was the attempt to assign the social groups themselves a fixed place as occupational estates in the organism of the state.

The Industrial Code (*Gewerbeordnung*) of the North German Confederation had eliminated all market-regulating corporations, craft guilds, and public monopolies in 1869 to clear the way completely for the principle of freedom of trade. Other corporations, such as the *Landesökonomie-Kollegium*, which was both a public umbrella organization of private farming associations and an advisory body of the state economic ministry, had lost their public character early under the sway of economic liberalism. This picture changed fundamentally as of the 1870s. At the beginning of the decade, the *Landesökonomie-Kollegium* regained its status. At the same time, laws strengthened the corporative components of the chambers of commerce by explicitly confirming their claim to represent the general interests of the industrial entrepreneur.[78] Artisans, too, pressed hard for restoration of "certain rights in the state organism," as their representatives put it.[79] Although the Imperial Industrial Code had retained the guilds, the restrictions it placed on all their corporative rights and privileges were interpreted by their members as heralding the eventual demise of their organizations. To the artisans, the "humiliation of discrimination and disempowerment" they decried lay primarily in the absence of the kind of "organic relations to the authorities" that the chambers of commerce had, and the most visible expression of those relations was the direct access to executive power.[80]

The artisans did not completely lose the struggle over their corporative reputation. In a decree of 4 January 1879, Bismarck expressly emphasized the importance of the guilds as agents of corporation rights and directed the governments of the empire's states to help create viable guilds. The Prussian chambers of industry (*Gewerbekammer*), too, owed their existence (scarcely successful though it was) mostly to the artisans' need for corporatist representation and integration. This demand was finally met in the Crafts Act of 1897, which not only introduced the "optional compulsory guild" (*fakultative Zwangsinnung*) but also provided for chambers of crafts as public corporations.[81] Chambers of Agriculture had been established three years earlier. The trend in the public organization of special interests thereby expanded beyond the classical chambers. It included two professional classes that had to protect themselves in a particular way against the dynamic of industrialization, and the successful representation of their interests also served the social stabilization of the Prussian state.

The impacts that this "chamberization" of important social groups had on the spread of corporative principles extended far beyond the system of chambers. Multiple institutional and personnel interconnections linked the private associations, too, with the system of institutionalized collaboration with state agencies. In 1897 chambers of commerce accounted for nearly one third of the member associations of the League of German Industry (*Centralverband Deutscher Industrieller*). In 1911 at least thirty-one of the fifty-three committee members of the German Trade Conference, a public-law association of chambers of commerce, were also members of the Hansa Federation for Commerce, Trade, and Industry (*Hansa-Bund für Gewerbe, Handel und Industrie*)—a private association. Conversely, half of all chambers of commerce belonged to the *Hansa-Bund* as corporative members.[82] Though outwardly impressive in number, conduct, and effect as pressure groups, the empire's private associations had little to do with the ideas of pluralistic interest intermediation. For the most part, they preferred the reassurance of organized cooperation with the authorities, which they enjoyed through interrelations with the chambers, and favored the possibility of direct access to executive power rather than the free competition of interests and work with parliament.

It may have been this high degree of autonomy and interconnectedness of the state and economic activity that hindered further formal institutionalization of the corporatist system. Such efforts had existed since the 1870s. In a period of crises and conflicts, they catered to a widespread yearning for harmony but also reflected the obvious necessity of stabilizing an economic system that had lurched out of control under the aegis of liberalism.

The rule of liberalism rested mostly on economic success. When that success disappeared and a long, deep depression ensued, German traditions of economic order almost inevitably resurfaced. Those who argued for organizing the state and society along state corporatist lines cited scholars such as George Wilhelm Friedrich Hegel (1770–1831), Johann Gottlieb Fichte (1762–1854), Friedrich Wilhelm Joseph Schelling (1775–1854), and Adam Müller (1779–1829). These thinkers had assigned public morality to the state and the corporation, not to the market; to the common interest, not to the individual. Hegel, above all, had little interest in an uncritical inventory of what existed, and even less in the nostalgic longing that many of his contemporaries felt for the glorious days of the past. Like Adam Smith (1723–1770), who had developed his idea of liberal capitalism's functioning before it ever actually existed, Hegel anticipated a socioeconomic development that lay far in the future. He was the first to ponder the growing complexity that industrialized society meant for the relationship between the individual, society, and the state and the first to contemplate that complexity's effect on the political system. With the category of "civil society," he introduced a link between the two poles represented by the individual and the state. To Hegel, it was the responsibility of the group to create within civil society the degree of cohesion that he considered necessary for the achievement of society's general objectives, even under the impending changes in economic conditions.

"Unless he is a member of a legitimate corporation," said Hegel in his critique of liberalism, "the individual is without professional honor, his isolation reduces his business to its selfish side, and his livelihood and satisfaction become insecure."[83] The task of the corporation within civil society was "to provide for the particular interest as a common interest"[84] and thereby return to public morality as something inherent in civil society. Hegel was too much a child of the Enlightenment and had too great an awareness of the economic and social change of his day to develop a rigid and static image of social inequality or to approve of an authoritarian political order. He did advocate privileges for corporations, but he also wanted them placed under "the higher supervision of the state because otherwise they would ossify, become complacent, and decline into a miserable system of castes."[85] According to Hegel, the privileges of the corporations were not to be regarded as arbitrary exceptions to universal law but rather as "legally created regulations owing to the nature of the special character inherent in an essential branch of society itself."[86] Based on this understanding of the corporation's responsibilities and regulations, the implications that Hegel derived for suffrage and the organization of popular representation were able to legitimate the corporatist model of representation:

> Deputies are sometimes regarded as "representatives"; but they are representatives in an organic, rational sense only if they are representatives not of individuals or

a conglomeration of them, but of one of the essential spheres of society and its large-scale interests. Hence representation cannot now be taken to mean simply the substitution of one man for another; the point is rather that the interest itself is actually present in its representative, while he himself is there to represent the objective element of his own being.[87]

To be sure, the antiparliamentary stance taken by Bismarck and other proponents of state corporatism did not stem solely from such considerations of principle. But without this backing from the tradition of German constitutional law and jurisprudence, the idea of reorganizing representation of economic interests along state corporatist lines after 1875 would not have attained the significance it did. Bismarck himself was prepared to subordinate isolated issues of his policies unconditionally to this objective. For example, the mandatory establishment of professional associations in the field of accident insurance was intended first and foremost to create patterns for reorganizing interest representation at the national level. Reporting about a discussion with Bismarck, the chancellor's closest associate on social policy, Theodor Lohmann, explained:

> Accident insurance in and of itself is secondary to him. The main thing to him in this connection is to arrive at corporate cooperative associations that would have to be set up gradually for all productive national classes so as to secure a basis for future representation of the people[. These cooperative associations] will become an essential contributing factor in legislation instead of or alongside the national parliament, even if in the extreme it takes a coup d'état.[88]

In addition to addressing the social question (to which the reorganization of interest mediation was a palliative), ensuring the national labor market's ability to function, and attending to labor, which was an ever more important factor of production, the fourth priority of the great social security project of the 1880s was to reorganize the representation of economic interests.

But the self-governing bodies of social security were not the only place where Bismarck's ideas of state corporatist representation of the people openly took shape. His notions always brushed the margins of constitutional legality as well—without, however, ever becoming "an essential contributing factor in legislation." The Prussian Economic Council (*Volkswirtschaftsrat*) appointed by royal order at the end of 1880 was meant as a preliminary step toward a "German economic senate." This German economic council was intended to subsume three existing umbrella organizations—the German Trade Conference, the League of German Industry, and the German Agricultural Council—into a "unified central organ" through which they would work together to balance the common and special interests of trade, industry, and agriculture.[89] Because the Reichstag refused to approve the budget for a national body, the Economic Council remained confined to Prussia. Even there, however, it led a shadowy political existence until its tacit dissolution in 1886. Bismarck kept it artificially alive without constitutional legitimization as of 1883 solely to make the point that he was continuing to pursue his plans.

The composition of its seventy-five members was consistent with the corporative principle. Forty-five of them were appointed from 120 candidates selected by the chambers of commerce, commercial corporations, and agricultural associations. In appointing the rest of the members, the ministries drew primarily on artisans and workers.[90] In this way, fifteen representatives of the artisan and working class, including three journeymen and three workers, took their seats in the council's section for industry and trade. Only one of the workers, the Berlin iron molder Friedrich Kamien, was a member of the union associations (Hirsch-Duncker). Men such as the councilor of commerce Louis Baare from Bochum and foreman Nikolaus Spengler from Mettlach, the spirits producer Albert Ernst from Halle an der Saale, the master mason Heinrich Beyerle from Coblenz, Count Guido Henckel von Donnersmark from Neudeck, and the factory worker Heinrich Kätsching from Itzehoe met in this section to deliberate jointly on accident insurance and the reorganization of the guilds. Given the selection procedure used,[91] it is no wonder that, "for all the differences of opinion, the political divergence between the parties never came to the fore" in the negotiations, as noted with the true ring of corporatist conviction in the 1881 annual report by the Bochum Chamber of Commerce.[92] Nevertheless—or precisely because of the antiparliamentary thrust of such views—the Prussian state diet finally rejected the budget of the Economic Council in a tie vote in 1883.

Despite the parliamentary defeat, the Prussian Economic Council persisted in its work for another three sessions, though without remuneration and reimbursement of costs. The cost issue had direct effects on the attendance of the fifteen members of the council on which the workers sat. Only five of them appeared for the 1884 term. Five of the absent members excused themselves expressly for lack of money.[93] Thus failed the first "top-down" attempt to integrate workers into the system of balancing interests in an organized way. At least the Prussian Economic Council, as the first organ of the Prussian state, regularly provided a few seats for representatives of the workers.

A bottom-up attempt to lend the council more weight likewise faltered. In 1884, the state government recommended the formation of chambers of industry, leaving both the election of members from trade, industry, agriculture, and the crafts and the appropriation of the necessary funds to the provincial associations. If the provincial diets were to reject the formation of chambers of industry, as happened in Westphalia, then so-called economic conferences of the four groups would be held at least at the district level. The government kept them on a tight rein, though. The regional presidents were allowed to raise for discussion only those questions that the ministry had approved beforehand. This tactic kept the really pressing matters of regional industry—transport and tariff issues, for example—off the agenda,[94] soon generating boredom and annoyance with consultation on problems about determining the weight of grain samples, the effects of convict labor on trade and industry, or the introduction of standard time.

In the cases where chambers of industry were created, the chambers of commerce overshadowed them from the outset. The resulting frustration in this area as well shone through in typical passages from the annual reports of the chambers: "The activity of the chamber of industry for the governmental district of Merseburg in 1888 focused primarily on the procurement of material for its annual report and its reimbursement. Continuous fruitful effectiveness through deliberation of important economic questions was, unfortunately, not permitted."[95]

There was no doubt in the late 1880s that Bismarck's project of reorganizing the representation of economic interests "according to a unified plan for the whole of the German Reich"[96] had completely foundered. It would be a mistake, however, to conclude that the rejection of corporatist counterparliaments meant an absence of corporatist structures in the German empire's policy on interest intermediation. In reality, the process of incorporating the private associations into the conservative social welfare system in Prussia and other German states was quite advanced. It occurred through interlinkage with the expanding chambers, through transfer of sovereign jurisdiction to nominally private associations, and through the orientation of the associations' functionaries to the image of state officials and the idea of the conservative welfare state. All that had miscarried in the Bismarckian design for a unified, macrosocial corporatist system was its authoritarian nature—and not least because corporatism in its liberal form (i.e., based on freedom of contract and coalition) had long pervaded the constitutional reality of the empire.

Cartels—Market Regulation German Style

The significance of cartels as a special manifestation of a general predilection for economic activity coordinated by associations dates back to the financial crash of 1873 and its aftermath. A cartel was unanimously defined by contemporaries around the turn of the twentieth century as a contractual (i.e., voluntary) association of independent enterprises, usually of the same kind, as a professional body of entrepreneurs whose objective was to control the market.[97] Unlike Adam Smith, who was convinced that "people of the same trade seldom meet together, even for merriment and diversion, but the conversation ends in conspiracy against the public," Gustav Schmoller saw "the moral significance" of coordinated market regulation in the fact that "it did not come about through purchase and foundings, the stock exchange and speculation, but rather through cooperative contract, through recognition of necessity, through the victory of common interests over self-interest and short-term egoism."[98] On behalf of a scientific community and a public that essentially accepted cartels, Schmoller thereby posed—and negated—the question of whether "the supreme economic principle is, and should remain, individual freedom, the free movement of all individual forces, whether the least constrained and most intense free competition is the most beneficial for economic development."[99]

Although the written version of the empire's economic order, the Industrial Code of 1869, continued to provide a liberal framework for economic activity in Germany, the cartels created a new mesoeconomic system of governance by concentrating market power and using new allocation mechanisms on the markets. Cartelization was a specifically German response to internal contradictions of the liberal economic doctrine. In reality, the better free competition functioned and the more it led to monopolistic or oligopolistic forms of the market, the less achievable ideal-type "complete competition" was. Faced with the choice between going down the road of trusts and following the U.S. example of consolidating entire economic sectors into market-dominating companies in which all participants lose their economic and legal independence, German entrepreneurs usually preferred coordinated regulation of the market. Whereas Werner Sombart noted all of four cartels in 1865,[100] Friedrich Kleinwächter, who "discovered" the expansion of cartelization in 1883 as a topic for science, reported that hardly any branch of big industry was likely to be without cartels.[101] Cartelization persisted during cyclical booms, too, prompting Max Weber to see it justifiably as a process whose significance in superior capitalist development went far beyond its function of affording mutual protection for entrepreneurs in times of crisis. Like the vast majority of his contemporaries, he moved away from the zeitgeist of the French Revolution, which was bent on destroying every kind of corporative structure. He elevated cartels, syndicates, and the like, along with their allocational function, to the constitutive principle of capitalist economic governance. In his opinion this revision satisfied "the economic needs of capitalism and, for the noncapitalist classes, the needs of the market economy."[102]

The reality of the German economy's structures around the turn of the century had in fact veered quite a bit from liberal economic postulates. As Schmoller unapologetically stated in a comment on the proceedings of the government's cartel investigation committee in 1902: "A good deal of the freedom of trade and the free competition of which we were so proud has been buried by the cartels, if not legally, then in fact."[103] However, the contradiction between how the economy was supposed to be governed and how it really was governed did not in the least slow the expansion of the cartels and their coordinated regulation of the market. Germany had become "the classical country of cartels"[104] even before the famous Imperial Court decision of 1897 that legalized this circumstance and thereby granted judicial protection and full legitimacy in private law to the coordinated market economy as the principle of German economic governance.

The Germany of Emperor William II—with its bureaucratic traditions and extensive administrative apparatus; its capitalist economic order of diverse "organized" agencies, that is, large corporations, cartels, syndicates, trade associations, unions, cooperative associations, chambers, umbrella associations, and economic councils; its coexistence of pluralistic, state corporatist, and liberal corporatist interest intermediation (with the latter two forms ever more pronounced)—this Germany bore the features of the coming twentieth century more than it did the onus of the old order.[105] A new type of capitalism and civil society was about to emerge at the end of the nineteenth century. Its departure from liberal principles of running an economy cannot be described as "late feudal" or as beholden to a preindustrial value system. That would mean overlooking the development toward a coordinated market economy that characterized the economic order of the coming century.

The unions, one of the three key pillars of postindustrial corporatism, were not yet included much in interest intermediation under the German empire. But one could already make out the organizational framework in which it became possible to integrate the working class, first under the aegis of war socialism and then under the democratic auspices of the Weimar Republic, without having to undergo a revolutionary upheaval of social conditions.

Societal Corporatism in the Weimar Republic

It has often been said that the dominance of organized interests within the Weimar Republic's early political, social, and economic life resulted from the weakness of the system's political bodies, a lack of liberal democratic tradition, and especially the tremendous pressure that the Great War and its immediate aftermath put on economic life. Although accurate, these observations do not sufficiently explain the clout and staying power of corporative organizational and decision-making mechanisms in the republic's economic and social policy. The challenge posed by the war economy, which most people in the labor movement did not wish to dodge,[106] only accelerated the collectivization of economic decision-making and the balancing of society's interests.

The first moves to expand the corporatist system of balancing interests into a durable net of associations suspended from three mainstays came from the unions soon after the war began.[107] The initiative to have labor and management form a united front passed to the employers in 1917 after the government compelled cooperation in the War Food Office, the Reich Economic Office, the War Office, the War Materials Allocation Division, and other central agencies. This momentum had gathered during the military social policy of the war years and after experience with the arbitration commissions and committees established by the Auxiliary Service Act of 5 December 1916, which granted labor and management equal representation. In October and

November 1918 it led to the formal recognition of the unions as parties to the industrial relations system. The Central Joint Labor-Management Board of Economic Planning and Regulation (*Zentralarbeitsgemeinschaft der industriellen und gewerblichen Arbeitgeber und Arbeitnehmer Deutschlands*, ZAG) was created in December of the same year.

Germany's plunge into total war in the autumn of 1916 called for methods of economic crisis management on a scale unnecessary in most other industrialized countries until the Great Depression of the early 1930s. But Germany, the land of cartels, associations, and chambers, was well equipped with the necessary measures. Inclusion of the unions in the cooperative framework of organized interests logically rounded out the system of liberal corporatism that had taken root in the prewar period. For that reason, the collaboration between capital and labor during and after World War I, though born of necessity, was not perceived only as a temporary expedient. Observers in the social democratic camp and the union movement who before the war had interpreted cartels and other collective and cooperative forms of organized capitalism as steps toward social democracy or even socialism[108] understood their own involvement now as the necessary and logical continuation and extension of this principle.

On the other side of the social spectrum, the entrepreneurs could retain a high degree of autonomy in the long run only if they succeeded in finding allies in rejecting calls for forms of a centrally controlled economy. Marxists were not the only ones raising such demands. Conservatives were looking in that direction, too, when they envisioned the creation of a state corporatist system modeled on Bismarck's ideal.[109] Granted, "when choosing between socialization on the one side and a planned economy on the other," it behooved a shrewd tactician of heavy industry "to walk a stretch with the proponents of the latter."[110] But the representatives of the northwest German coal, iron, and steel industry resisted. They in particular stood to be affected by the plans for a common economy drawn up by the head of the Ministry of Economics, Rudolf Wissell, and his undersecretary, Wichard von Moellendorff. The industrialists knew from the outset that it could not lie in their interest "to head once and for all down the path to a common economy (*Gemeinwirtschaft*), which ... leads to socialization" and which to them meant "compulsory regulation and perpetual government control."[111] The entrepreneurs thus had only one potent ally, the workers. Against this backdrop the entrepreneurs, too, saw that ZAG had the prospect of becoming more than a short-lived pact between capital and labor to ward off bureaucratization, parliamentary control, and revolution.

ZAG thoroughly succeeded in this respect, all in all benefiting the working class as well.[112] Nevertheless, it suffered from a critical congenital defect. The compromise on economic and social policy, specifically wage policy, rested on the shifting sands of inflationary conditions. Inflation allowed liabilities created by compromises to be passed on to third parties, at least until

1923, a possibility that freed the industrial partners from pressure to stipulate the material conditions of the Weimar Republic at a level that both sides were willing to accept on a long-term basis. At the end of the inflationary period— or more accurately, during the phase of hyperinflation, when monetary depreciation lost it tranquilizing, irenic function—this flaw left ZAG bereft of its basis for doing business. Hyperinflation weighed heavily upon ZAG, and the entrepreneurs blamed the organization for what they considered the untenable and excessive burden placed on the republic's economy by the redistributional effects of wage and social policy.

ZAG's jurisdiction in this situation was nearly all-encompassing. According to the statutes of the organization, its purpose was to arrive at "a common solution to all economic and sociopolitical issues touching upon Germany's industry and trade and to all legislative and administrative matters."[113] When ZAG was dissolved on 31 March 1924, it still had the right to appoint some of the members of the National Potash Council, the National Coal Council, the foreign trade offices, the Iron Industry Federation (*Eisenwirtschaftsbund*, an organization in which industrialists, unions, and consumers collaborated to regulate iron sales), the Electricity Industry Advisory Board, the Standing Exhibition for Workers' Welfare, the Workers' Headquarters (which was responsible for the recruitment of foreign workers from abroad), the Prussian Industry and Trade Supervisory Service, and the National Economic Council, which was provided for by Article 165 of the Weimar constitution and "provisionally" established in 1920. As a purely advisory and assessment body, the Provisional National Economic Council had only very limited capacity to assume and continue ZAG functions. But the council did offer an institutional platform for cooperation, which usually had an informal, symbolic, but in some cases also demonstrative, character.

The end of the inflationary period brought the need to formulate a new, albeit less institutionalized, basis for cooperation between capital and labor. But the economic aberrations and distributional battles after World War I made such renegotiation among the vested interests just as impossible as it was necessary. Since 1922, the unions had seen themselves confronted with the demand of the entrepreneurs to review the material constitution of Weimar, so they vociferously decried the attack on the foundations of the "historical compromise" of 1918–1919. The demands of the leading industrialists to reexamine the status quo went far indeed. In a draft program for the "reconstruction of the German economy" (26 December 1922),[114] Paul Silverberg, the chairman of the Rhine Lignite Syndicate (*Rheinisches Braunkohlesyndikat*, or Rheinbraun Syndicate) and a member of the presiding committee of the Reich Association of German Industry (*Reichsverband der Deutschen Industrie*, RDI), called for nothing less than a strike ban and severe limitations on the right of collective wage bargaining and the right of association. Yet even at this early point, the draft was rejected within the association and by the government of Reich Chancellor Wilhelm Cuno (1922–1923), who had close ties to the business community as the former head of the Hamburg-American Shipping Line (HAPAG). Responding to Silverberg's proposal, the national government called the "exaggeration of his demands ... in various places outright grotesque."[115] By contrast, representatives of the New Industries, including the managing director of the Federation of the German Electrical Engineering Industry, Hans von Raumer, still wanted "to reinvigorate the Joint Labor-Management Board" and "to handle our problems jointly with union representatives," all with an eye to raising productivity and the number of working hours.[116]

Even without a successor to ZAG, however, the relative prosperity that prevailed from 1925 to late 1929 enabled the workers to win back some of the ground they had first gained during the years of revolution and inflation and had then lost during hyperinflation and the stabilization crisis. In 1927 they achieved the hotly disputed eight-hour workday and the reinstatement of the three-shift system in the iron industry. They also secured relatively favorable real wages and scored new successes in wage and social policy, which the unions, as the very spirit of the labor movement (*Geist von ihrem Geiste*),[117] attributed to their own effectiveness. Prime examples of these advances include the rise in public spending on housing; the expansion of social security, namely, the introduction of unemployment insurance (1927); and, in labor law, the Labor Court Act of 1926, which led to the establishment of the National Labor Court the following year.

These triumphs came within a tripartite, interest-balancing, abidingly corporatist system in which, however, the state increasingly became the mainstay, as evidenced by its growing involvement in wage policy. The focus of policy on interest intermediation during the Weimar Republic shifted from direct disputes between the industrial partners to the national minister of labor. He assumed "leadership functions"[118] far beyond those of a mediator primarily through the way he used his authority to end labor disputes by declaring a collective bargaining proposal binding. He thereby brought an authoritative element into the process of balancing interests. The unions profited from the labor movement's interconnections, which extended from the workers' parties through the Center Party to the conservatives, the German National People's Party (DNVP). This range made the unions politically important enough to obtain concessions in various coalitions from National Labor Minister Heinrich Brauns, who held office until 1928 and who was close to the Christian unions.

The unions believed that intervention by the state, which at that time was governed mostly by the Center Party, the Liberals, and the Nationalists rather than by the Social Democrats, Communists, or National Socialists (Nazis), gave the necessary protection from the dictatorship of the market. The business community, however, was interested in further developing the cooperative framework of interest intermediation only if the distribution of power changed. In this context, Paul Silverberg's Dresden speech of 4 September 1926[119] reads like an attempt to reclaim the initiative on interest intermediation so as to make something of the economy's now enhanced importance in close cooperation with the unions. Against the backdrop of a secret initiative of the General Federation of Unions (ADGB), which included weekly "informal meetings" with representatives of the RDI early in 1926, Silverberg called for recognition "that salvation for Germany and Germany's economy lay only in trustful cooperation with German labor and that, on this basis, broad groups of German industrialists have the courage to conclude that the political cooperation and joint responsibility of the Social Democratic Party must be a goal."[120]

As plainly indicated by the storm of controversy over Silverberg's words at that early time, the business leaders had immense difficulty formulating a binding offer of cooperation, if any at all. Such initiatives, which came mostly from the ranks of export-centered New Industries, encountered the mounting veto power of heavy industry, whose waxing influence on the tone of industrial interest policy[121] was burdening each overture for more cooperation with conditions unacceptable to employees. The will to cooperate that still existed in chemicals, machine manufacturing, electrical engineering, automotive manufacturing, and other New Industries even after the failure of ZAG also ran into the resistance of those RDI associations in which small business was organized. Companies in that category feared that consensus within big business could come at their expense. It was therefore no accident that the Association of Saxon Industrialists counted among the instigators of the opposition in the dissention over Silverberg's speech.

Not even the dire straits of the Great Depression in the early 1930s, which led to corporatist forms of interest intermediation in other nations, too—even in Great Britain and the United States[122]—could revive the old intensity of cooperation in Germany. On the contrary, more and more companies saw looming mass unemployment as leverage with which to challenge the social governance of the Weimar Republic, which they made out to be the principal cause of the grave crisis in Germany. This burden weighed upon each attempt to come up with a mutually agreed-upon alternative strategy for economic policy and to revive the idea of ZAG, practically condemning every effort to futility from the start.

This constellation had its counterpart in the unions as well. Since the days of hyperinflation in 1923, the labor movement's rank and file had a deeply rooted distrust of a ZAG policy that they blamed for many missed opportunities of the revisionist course steered by labor in the early years of the republic and the one pursued by employers. Every attempt to revive the Joint Labor-Management Board would therefore have initially strengthened the "revolutionary opposition" within the unions. Moreover, the social balance of power had meanwhile definitely shifted in favor of the entrepreneurs. Holding a relatively weak position, many functionaries of the union movement therefore felt it too risky to allow themselves to be incorporated into a joint economic and sociopolitical concept that was bound to show the hand of the business community even more clearly than just a few years earlier. These motives lurked in the background when the ADGB leadership immediately tried to quash every nascent suspicion about a return to superordinate organized forms of cooperation with the RDI, repeatedly emphasizing: "We hardly need to assure our union members that we reject any kind of joint labor-management board."[123]

Given the crisis faced by the two camps, however, the representatives of big business and labor did not doubt each other's good will to enter into at least partial communities of interest.[124] The employers' presentiments that "the terrible situation demands [this] ... if things are not to disintegrate completely"[125] sounded similar to appraisals by the ADGB leadership: "May the unions withdraw from involvement in direct negotiations with the employers when the national parliament and the government seem stymied in attempts to find a solution, when incalculable misery threatens to break over the economy and labor?"[126] But as much as both sides wanted to publicly demonstrate at least minimal practical cooperation in the shadow of crisis, the attempts they made to have their own constituencies accept the idea tended to reveal the powerlessness of politically farsighted interest mediators to fend off the impending disaster.

There was no lack of such effort. In May and June 1930, before the nadir of the crisis, negotiations between an RDI commission, and the German Employers' League (*Vereinigung der Deutschen Arbeitgeberverbände*, VDA), and the ADGB were opened in order to formulate a statement on the principles of future economic, social, and finance policy. By late May the two camps had already agreed to declare "a firm commitment to maintain our social legislation as far as the performance of the German economy permits," "to maintain a balanced budget under all circumstances," "to accept spending reductions over the development of new sources of revenues," to maintain unemployment insurance, to request a "special crisis premium" from higher-income employees and civil servants, "to discount production costs, and to lower commodity prices."[127] The statement clearly shows the hand of the new chancellor, Heinrich Brüning, who worked with Labor Minister Adam Stegerwald on the first draft submitted by the employers and who took part in the first confidential round of negotiations.[128]

The joint resolution marks the beginning of the broad deflation-centered consensus that rested politically on the parliamentary foundation of the Brüning administration—including the Social Democrats and the unions. It was certainly not about formulaic entreaties of a worn-out finance policy whose survival and subsequent serious exacerbation of the crisis were due to ignorance of alternative strategies. The political elite of the Weimar Republic had acquired a good deal of practice at deficit spending to overcome cyclical drops in employment. The annual national budgets from 1919 through 1922 reflected such effects by having prevented the world economic crisis of 1920 from spreading to Germany. The government acted with particular resolve during the recession of 1925–1926, when it lowered taxes, supported exports, increased funding for housing projects, and raised public spending and relief work across the board—all pump-priming measures that had to be financed on credit.[129] But whereas 1927 already showed signs of an upturn, the financial burden of the experiment for overcoming the crisis continued to drag upon the economy and seriously narrowed the national government's maneuvering room on matters of financial and reparations policy. The experience of 1925 and 1926 therefore confirmed the employers, employees, and their representative organizations in their skepticism of the new policy of trying to counteract downturns in the business cycle by means of deficit spending. Whether believing in the power of the market to right itself or in the Marxist position that these events serve to cleanse the system and devalue capital, all the actors saw a reinforcement of the classical perspective on the functions that cyclical crises of overproduction have in capitalism. This basic consensus on economic and financial policy paved the way for practical cooperation between the parties of the industrial relations system.

Nevertheless, it never came to a joint declaration that the president of the republic was intended to read in order to lend it additional weight. The draft first encountered resistance from leading members of the RDI and the VDA, who, like Hermann Bücher of AEG (Allgemeine Elektricitäts-Gesellschaft), the major German electronics and electrical equipment manufacturer, called for a "fundamental change of the system" as they understood it (i.e., "the return to the capitalist system"). Others, such as Ernst von Borsig, noted the absence of an „equivalent for the huge sacrifices made by business."[130] Ultimately, the opposition in the employers' camp did not muster enough support for specific demands, such as the call to suspend authority to declare decisions of wage arbitration binding. But in a second draft of the statement, the employers did succeed at watering down the commitment to maintain the level of real wages and at souring the subsequent negotiations[131] to the point that the unions did not want to accept the statement. This turn of events had no impact on the policy of informal cooperation in the top echelon of the associations or on the Social Democrats' toleration of Brüning's policies. If there was behind-the-scenes talk of bringing back the grand coalition as early as May 1930, the RDI called for it with even greater urgency after the national elections in September, which handed the Nazi party 107 seats in the Reichstag.[132]

Negotiations resumed in October, with the initiative taken by the RDI leadership in May and June now passing to Labor Minister Stegerwald, who as early as February 1930 had advocated the "restoration of ZAG."[133] He had modeled his interest intermediation on the corporative ideas of Catholic social doctrine.[134] But the renewed sally stemmed also from obvious political and pragmatic motives. As politically averse as Brüning was to a coalition with the Social Democrats, it was important for his government to win the support of the industrial partners for its ever more unpopular concept of deflationary interventions in the economy. Given the broad agreement on the principles of this policy, the goal definitely seemed achievable.

By the end of this round of negotiations on 9 December 1930, there did indeed exist a catalogue of shared principles[135] grounded in the general consensus on deflation. Whereas the employers' associations, the Christian union (which was more corporatist than the ADGB), the Hirsch-Duncker unions (which were more liberal than the ADGB), and the federal managing board of the ADGB approved the statement (the ADGB, by a vote of eight to three), the ADGB members' committee voted against it by a large majority, thwarting open cooperation with the employers. The representatives of the various unions criticized mainly the obligation "to change union contracts immediately through amicable settlement" if "mutual agreement" had been reached, and they demanded abstention from "every avoidable termination of collective agreements."[136] Their rejection emanated also from the surely not unjustified fear that the entrepreneurs might be pursuing a two-track strategy of seeking cooperation at the top level, but confrontation on the shop floor. With the Weimar democratic system in danger of collapsing, those arguing in favor of the declaration were less concerned with its substance than with its political effect. As stressed by the leader of the Social Democratic faction in the Reichstag, Otto Wels, "a large bloc of extraordinary political significance would be created between the unions and employers' associations."[137] The chairman of the woodworkers' union, Fritz Tarnow, viewed "an agreement with business leaders as a temporary marriage of convenience" that was useful because it was likely "that we will be on the verge of dictatorship in the foreseeable future."[138]

Establishment of a common front for combating the exigency would probably have had little effect on the economic facts in 1930–1931, for both camps stood firmly by the concept of deflationary intervention.[139] It would have become decisive for simultaneously overcoming the crisis and retaining a democratic system. But in 1931–1932 the outlines of an effective strategy for dealing with the situation finally became apparent, and the reservations about using it gradually yielded to the escalating pressure of the republic's problems.

The turning point seemed to have come in December 1931 and in January and March 1932, when the Central Committee on Raising Production, especially through Job Creation, which the Provisional National Economic Council had set up in August 1931, came to grips with the country's economic state of emergency. At last it was accepted that the "world crisis ... [could] no longer be thought of in terms of parallels with the normal cyclical crises that periodically shook the world economy, particularly the economies of the highly industrialized countries, in the final decades of peace and yet always led out of the effects of the crisis and again back to recovery and a new ascent."[140]

This realization of the dire nature of the country's condition instilled the willingness to switch from indirect to direct measures of cyclical policy by means of public job creation. The Provisional National Economic Council duly proposed job creation costing between 1.2 to 1.8 billion Reichmarks (RM), to be financed on credit, a move with which the council hoped to send up to 855,000 people back to work.[141] Although the scale of the National Economic Council's job-creation program does not seem great enough to dent the crisis seriously, it did go well beyond the approaches that the national government had considered up to that time. But despite the fact that the Provisional National Economic Council proportionately represented Germany's economic and social forces, it did not have the authority of a great block between unions and employers' associations. Only that backing could have imbued it with the political clout necessary to push through an expansive strategy for coping with the crisis democratically. The resistance to it was considerable and extended from the Reichsbank to the entrepreneurs. In the end, only the authoritarian option seemed feasible.

The liberal-corporatist system of German interest intermediation faced an almost unsolvable problem. During World War I, a relatively extensive institutional basis for cooperation between the industrial partners had formed, a foundation that had been crucial for the republic's political and social stabilization, particularly during the years of demobilization and inflation. Postwar Germany, however, was confronted by a number of extraordinarily difficult political, social, and economic problems that would surely have overwhelmed any system for balancing interests.

In this situation, the business community did not see itself in a long-term position to sustain the material constitution that had been achieved by working closely with the unions. To the captains of business, all the adversity of the economy's internal and external development was concentrated in the workers' new power and influence on distribution. To the workers, every demand for change by the employers jeopardized essential foundations of the republic. Until the last moment, it seemed quite possible at the top level to balance interests. But a strong minority hostile to cooperation forced both sides to put tactical considerations before acknowledgment of the benefits that trust and cooperation would have. The more necessary it became to reach a consensus in order to survive the challenge of the Great Depression democratically, the less acceptable that compromise was to each side. The remarkable thing was thus not so much the complete breakdown of cooperation in the Great Depression but rather the fact that this setback gave rise to authoritarian forms of corporatist interest intermediation rather than a revival of liberal-corporatist economic practices.

The foes of open cooperation with the unions came primarily from heavy industry, which had long since broken with liberal economic principles. But the crisis also strengthened opposition to economic liberalism among those who considered themselves the victims of the interplay between the strong labor movement and big industry. They felt disadvantaged by the rules of Weimar interest intermediation, the most general manifestation of which was the primacy of the economy. These groups believed that they could protect themselves more effectively with government assistance than with the major economic and social organizations. Whether in its old form of self-employed artisans and merchants, small businessmen, and overindebted farmers or in its new guise of status-seeking officials and employees, the weakly organized middle class saw its legitimate interests crushed between the two powerful blocs: the unions and big industry. The members of this group not only blamed the Weimar Republic's liberal corporatism for the wage-and-price spiral, the main burden of which fell upon the middle class in their estimation. They also linked the cartel of capital and labor to the continuing concentration of industry, the dramatic decline in the number of the self-employed, and other long-term macroeconomic structural changes that the middle class felt imperiled by.

This dissatisfaction finally culminated in a grass-roots uprising against the capitalist marketplace, as Charles S. Maier aptly describes the situation.[142] Although the marketplace had long ceased being the most important arena of economic decision-making, there is no denying the impulse of anticapitalism behind this rebellion. Its thrust was aimed at the ever more disquieting, tacit, albeit conflict-ridden, dual supremacy of big industry and the unions, which ruled over the economic fate of the "unorganized" middle class—illegitimately, as the members of that social group saw it. Unable to defy this cartel economically, the rebels preferred the primacy of politics. A system in which the government had the leading role in balancing interests was expected to better accommodate the economically weak, organizationally fragmented, and thus heretofore disadvantaged groups. The proposed policies of the Third Reich seemed consistent with these notions.

The triumph and failure of the corporative balancing of interests sealed the fate of the Weimar Republic in two senses. Without the alliance between the labor movement and the industrial middle class, post-1918 Germany threatened to sink into the chaos of civil war. The Weimar Republic, with the chance it offered to continue democratic development of economic dynamics, build the welfare state, and achieve policy goals in which the empire had placed hope, depended on cooperation between capital and labor if it wanted to survive under onerous political conditions at home and abroad. Disappointment with liberal corporatist balancing of interests and the termination of the historic compromise of 1918–1919 in response to the dual challenge of the Great Depression and the rise of Hitler's movement thus ensured the first republic's demise long before the National Socialists seized power in January 1933.

The interest intermediation of the coordinated market economy did not perish with the Weimar Republic any more than the social system of production did. The corporatist approach to balancing interests, however, did lack autonomous actors for a few years after 1945 because the occupation powers were very hesitant about agreeing to revitalize the associations, which had been brought under the total control of the Nazi regime. But the first real post-war challenge that the resurgence of the West German economy encountered, the Korean crisis of the 1950s, resuscitated old patterns of corporatist interest intermediation. Trade associations—and to a lesser extent the unions as well—assumed tasks of the national government, closing the control gap that the early concept of the social market economy left open in the economic policy of the Federal Republic of Germany. In principle, the primacy of politics continued, but the vested economic interests succeeded at becoming so intensely involved again in the formulation of economic policy that critics called to mind the "rule of the associations" (Theodor Eschenburg) to describe the re-empowerment of organized interests in West German interest intermediation in the long 1950s.

The Grand Coalition (1966–1969) ultimately brought this development back into the formal course of political decision-making, whose locus thereby shifted still further from parliament.[143] It moved to the round tables of concerted action staged by political actors in the tradition of Weimar interest intermediation in an effort to eliminate the backlog of reforms that had built during the Adenauer era. Like the economy itself, the vision of successful interest intermediation did not follow the paradigm of conflict and its contentious resolution. Instead, it set store by consensus and cooperation among the associations, with the job of facilitation falling to the political community as a matter of course. If attention turned to the German model in the 1970s, particularly outside the country, it focused not least on the promise of social equalization and political stability that seemed inherent in this mode of interest intermediation. As long as the coordinated market economy appealed to the collective reason of the actors and bridged the polarities of interests through consensus, it proved superior. At the same time, however, that system's limitations stand out clearly against the historical experiences with the Great Depression of the early 1930s. The contrast is worth keeping in mind, especially since the current constellation of interest intermediation—unlike the present economic configuration—is in some ways strikingly reminiscent of the abortive "Alliance for Work" of the early 1930s.

Notes

1. Report to Talleyrand on 13 August 1799, in Paul Bailleu (Ed.), *Preußen und Frankreich von 1795 bis 1807: Diplomatische Correspondenzen, Erster Teil* (Osnabrück: Zeller, 1965; reprint of the 1881 edition), p. 505.

2. Werner Abelshauser, "Freiheitlicher Korporatismus im Kaiserreich und in der Weimarer Republik," in Werner Abelshauser (Ed.), *Die Weimarer Republik als Wohlfahrtsstaat: Zum Verhältnis von Wirtschafts- und Sozialpolitik in der Industriegesellschaft* (Stuttgart: Steiner, 1987), p. 159.

3. Hans-Ulrich Wehler, *Deutsche Gesellschaftsgeschichte 1849–1914* (Munich: Beck, 1995), p. 1266.

4. On the economic foundation of the knowledge society, see Daniel Bell, *The Coming of Post-Industrial Society: A Venture in Social Forecasting* (New York: Basic Books, 1973). See also Radovan Richta, *Richta-Report: Politische Ökonomie des 20. Jahrhunderts* (Frankfurt am Main: Makol, 1971) and Peter F. Drucker, *Post-Capitalist Society* (New York: HarperBusiness, 1993). On the relationship between globalization and the knowledge society, see James Brian Quinn, *Intelligent Enterprise: A Knowledge and Service Based Paradigm for Industry* (New York: The Free Press, 1992), p. 220.

5. James N. Rosenau, *Turbulence in World Politics: A Theory of Change and Continuity* (New York: Harvester Wheatsheaf, 1990).

6. David Harvey, *The Condition of Postmodernity: An Inquiry into the Origins of Cultural Change* (Oxford, England: Blackwell, 1989), ch. 9.

7. Richard Tilly, *Globalisierung aus historischer Sicht und das Lernen aus der Geschichte* (Cologne: Forschungsinstitut für Sozial- und Wirtschaftsgeschichte an der Universität zu Köln, 1999), p. 4. See also Kevin H. O'Rourke and Jeffrey G. Williamson, *Globalization and History: the Evolution of a Nineteenth Century Atlantic Economy,* (Cambridge, MA: MIT 1999) and Knut Borchardt, *Globalisierung in historischer Perspektive* [Bayerische Akademie der Wissenschaften, Philosophisch-historische Klasse—Sitzungsberichte—Jahrgang 2001, Heft 2] (Munich: Beck, 2001). For a more cautious, but similar, orientation, see Michael D. Bordo, Barry Eichengreen, and Douglas A. Irwin, "Is globalization today really different than globalization a hundred years ago?" (NBER Working Paper Series 7195) Cambridge, MA, 1999, p. 3.

8. See, for example, Mira Wilkins (Ed.), *The Growth of Multinationals* (Aldershot, England: Elgar, 1991).

9. Mira Wilkins and Harm G. Schröter, *The Free-Standing Company in the World Economy, 1830–1996* (Oxford, England: Oxford University Press, 1999).

10. John Foreman-Peck, *A History of the World Economy: International Economic Relations since 1850* (Brighton: Harvester Press, 1983); Wolfram Fischer (Ed.), *The Emergence of a World Economy, 1500–1914* (Wiesbaden: Steiner, 1986).

11. August Sartorius von Waltershausen, *Das volkswirtschaftliche System der Kapitalanlage im Ausland* (Berlin: Georg Reimer, 1907), p. 2.

12. Mira Wilkins, *The History of Foreign Investment in the United States to 1914* (Cambridge, MA: Harvard University Press, 1989), p. 145.

13. Horst Siebert, "Disziplinierung der internationalen Wirtschaftspolitik durch die internationale Kapitalmobilität," in Dieter Duwendag (Ed.), *Finanzmärkte im Spannungsfeld von Globalisierung, Regulierung und Geldpolitik*, Schriften des Vereins für Socialpolitik, vol. 261, pp. 41–67 (Berlin: Duncker & Humblot: 1998), p. 43.

14. Wilkins, *History*, p. 625.

15. See Werner Abelshauser, "Staat, Infrastruktur und interregionaler Wohlstandsausgleich im Preußen der Hochindustrialisierung," in Fritz Blaich (Ed.), *Staatliche Umverteilungspolitik in historischer Perspektive: Beiträge zur Entwicklung des Staatsinterventionismus in Deutschland und Österreich*, Schriften des Vereins für Socialpolitik, New Series, vol. 109 (Berlin: Duncker & Humblot, 1980), pp. 9–58.

16. Joseph A. Schumpeter, *Business Cycles: A Theoretical, Historical, and Statistical Analysis of the Capitalist Process*, vol. 1 (New York: McGraw Hill, 1939), ch. 7, section E.

17. See, for example, Heinrich August Winkler, *Pluralismus oder Protektionismus? Verfassungspolitische Probleme des Verbandswesens im deutschen Kaiserreich*, Vorträge des Instituts für Europäische Geschichte, vol. 55 (Wiesbaden: Steiner, 1972); Werner Abelshauser, "The first post-liberal nation: Stages in the development of modern corporatism in Germany," *European History Quarterly*, 14/3 (1984), 285–318.

18. Karl Fischer, *Grundzüge einer Sozialpädagogik und Sozialpolitik* (Eisenach: Wilkens, 1893), p. 6.

19. Siegfried Tschierschky, "Neumerkantilismus und wirtschaftliche Interessenorganisation," *Schmollers Jahrbuch*, 37 (1913), p. 18.

20. Siegfried Tschierschky, *Kartell und Trust* (Göttingen: Vandenhoeck & Ruprecht, 1903), p. 56.

21. Hans Rosenberg, *Große Depression und Bismarckzeit* (Berlin: Walter de Gruyter, 1967), p. 60.

22. Ibid.

23. Ibid.

24. Thorstein Veblen, *Imperial Germany and the Industrial Revolution* (Ann Arbor: University of Michigan Press, 1968), pp. 270–271. (Original work published 1915)

25. See especially David P. Calleo, *Legende und Wirklichkeit der deutschen Gefahr: Neue Aspekte zur Rolle Deutschlands in der Weltgeschichte von Bismarck bis heute* (Bonn: Keil, 1980) and David Blackbourn and Geoff Eley, *The Peculiarities of German History: Bourgeois Society and Politics in Nineteenth-Century Germany* (Oxford, England: Oxford University Press, 1984). For a summary, see Bernd Faulenbach, "'Deutscher Sonderweg': Zur Geschichte und Problematik einer zentralen Kategorie des deutschen geschichtlichen Bewußtseins," *Aus Politik und Zeitgeschichte*, B33 (1981), 3–21. On the revisionism of the Bielefeld School, see Hans-Ulrich Wehler, *Deutsche Gesellschaftsgeschichte 1849–1914* (Munich: Beck, 1995), pp. 449–486, and idem, "Artikel 'Sonderwegsdebatte'," in Michael Behnen (Ed.), *Lexikon der deutschen Geschichte 1945–1990* (Stuttgart: Kröner, 2002), pp. 531–534.

26. Geoff Eley, "Capitalism and the Wilhelmine state: Industrial growth and political backwardness in recent German historiography, 1890–1918," *Historical Journal*, 21 (1978), p. 741.

27. See Dick Geary, "Arbeiter und Unternehmer im deutschen Kaiserreich," in Werner Abelshauser (Ed.), *Konflikt und Kooperation. Strategien europäischer Gewerkschaften im 20. Jahrhundert* (Essen: Klartext, 1988), pp. 170–183.

28. See Charles Gross, *The Gild Merchant*, 2 vols. (Oxford, England: Clarendon Press, 1890).

29. See Gross, *Gild*, ch. 8; Toulmin Smith, *English Gilds* (with an introductory essay by Lujo Brentano) (Oxford, England: Oxford University Press, 1870); William Ashley, *An Introduction to English Economic History and Theory, Part I* (London: Longman, Green & Co, 1888), ch. 2; William Cunningham, *The Growth of English Industry and Commerce during the Early and Middle Ages*, 5th ed. (Cambridge, England: Cambridge University Press, 1915), pp. 336–352. (Original work published 1882); Georg Brodnitz, *Englische Wirtschaftsgeschichte* (Handbuch der Wirtschaftsgeschichte), vol. 1, pp. 145–158 (Jena: Gustav Fischer, 1918).

30. See George Unwin, *The Gilds and Companies of London*, 4th ed. (London: Frank Cass & Co, 1963), pp. 63–65. (Original work published 1908)

31. Mary Dormer Harris (Ed.), *Coventry Leet Book*, Early English Text Society, vol. CXXXIV [134] Oxford, England: Oxford University Press, 1907), p. 32.

32. "Wir die meystir gewandmechir zu Frankenford, die dun kunt unsern herren, den scheffen und dem rade gemeynlich unse gewonheid und unse bescheidenheit, die wir von alder gehabit han . . ." Johann Friedrich Boehmer, *Urkundenbuch der Reichsstadt Frankfurt a. M.* (Glashütten im Taunus: Auvermann, 1901–1905), p. 635. (Original work published 1836)

33. See Otto von Gierke, *Das deutsche Genossenschaftsrecht*, vol. 1 (Darmstadt: Wissenschaftliche Buchgesellschaft, 1954), § 38. (Original work published 1868)

34. Boehmer, *Urkundenbuch*, p. 635.

35. 37, Edw. III, c. VI (*Statutes at Large* II, p. 163).

36. *Politische Discurs, von den eigentlichen Ursachen/deß Auff- und Abnehmens der Städt/Länder und Republicken etc,* unchanged reprint of the 3rd ed. (Glashütten im Taunus: Auvermann, 1972), p. 115. (Original work published 1688)

37. See Charles Mathew Clode, *Memorials of the Guild of Merchant Taylors of the Fraternity of St. John the Baptist in the City of London, and of Its Associated Charities and Institutions, Compiled and Selected by the Master of the Company for the Year 1873/4* (London: Harrison & Sons, 1875), pp. 3–7.

38. 15, Henry VI, c. VI (*Statutes* III), p. 216.

39. "Wolt man aber innen werden, daß Stet gut würden, und jederman dem andern getrew wer, so thet man Zünfft ab ." Johann Christian Lünig, *Des Teutschen Reichs=Archivs Partis Generalis etc. Continuatio II, Abt. CXC: Kaysers Sigismundi Reformation des Weltlichen und Policey=Wesens im Heiligen Römischen Reiche (1438 oder 1439)* (Leipzig: Lanck, 1720), Ch. IV: "Von den Zünfften in den Stetten," p. 239.

40. See Gross, *Gild*, p. 52.

41. 5, Elizabeth I, c. IV, in *Statutes* VI, pp. 159–175.

42. *Politische Discurs,* p. 115.

43. ". . . mit dem Vorbehalt ihnen gegeben [wurde] daß ihren Obern, darunter sie wohnhaftig, freystehe, diesselben nach gelegenheit der leuft und zeit zu ändern, zu erkleren, zu mehren oder zu wenigern." Christian Otto Mylius (Ed.), *Corpus Constitutionum Marchicarum, V. Teil: Von Polizey= Hochzeit= Kindtauffen= Begräbnis= und Trauer= Kleider= auch Feuer= Gassen= und andern zur Polizey gehörigen Ordnungen etc., Berlin 1740,* II. Abt., X. Cap., No. I: Ordnung von verschiedenen Puncten in Handwercks=Sachen, Sonnabend nach Martini 1541, Sp. 581.

44. "Was bey denn Innungen für undencklichen Jahren eingeführet, und insbesonderheit was Zucht und Ehrbarkeit betrifft, solches seind Wir in seinem vigore zulaßen gndst. Gesonnen." Mylius, *Corpus Constitutionum Marchicarum, VI. Teil: Landtages=Recesse, von Justitzien= Zoll= Brau= und anderen Sachen etc. Berlin 1751,* No. CXVIII: Landtages=Receß, dd. 26. Jul. 1653, Sp. 458.

45. Mylius, *Corpus Constitutionum Marchicarum,* V. Teil: II. Abt., X. Cap., No. XVII: Verordnung an die Lehns=Cantzley, daß die Zünffte und Handwercker nicht mehr gewisse Anzahlen derer Meister haben sollen, Sp. 646.

46. "Kayserliche Majestät und das Reich [dörfften] leicht Gelegenheit nehmen . . . , nach dem Beyspiel anderer Reiche, und damit das Publicum durch dergleichen freventliche Privat-Händel in Zukunfft nicht ferner gehemmet oder belästiget werde, alle Zünffte insgesamt und überhaupt völlig aufzuheben und abzuschaffen." Reichs=Schluß wegen Abstellung der Unordnungen und Mißbräuche bey den Handwerkern, dd. 16. Aug. 1731, in Johann Andreas Ortloff (Ed.), *Corpus Juris Opificiarii,* pp. 3–28 (Erlangen: Schubart, 1804), p. 26.

47. Mylius, *Corpus Constitutionum Marchicarum,* V. Teil: II. Abt., X. Cap., Anhang: "Die General - Privilegia und Gülde - Briefe derer in der Chur und Marck Brandenburg dis= und jenseits der Oder und Elbe befindlichen Zünffte und Handwercke etc." The standardization characterizing the reform of craft-related legislation comes through even more clearly in Baden. See "Badische Allgemeine Zunftordnung, wornach sich bey allen Zünften, soweit nicht die Art der Treibung des Handwerks oder andere Hindernisse entgegenstehen, zu richten, dd. Carlsruhe, am 25sten October 1760," in Ortloff, *Corpus Juris Opificiarii,* pp. 225–247.

48. Gustav Schmoller, *Umrisse und Untersuchungen zur Verfassungs-, Verwaltungs- und Wirtschaftsgeschichte, besonders des preußischen Staates im 17. und 18. Jahrhundert* (Leipzig: Duncker & Humblot, 1898), p. 447.

49. Gustav Schmoller, *Zur Geschichte der deutschen Kleingewerbe im 19. Jahrhundert* (Halle: Waisenhaus, 1870), pp. 307, 665.

50. See Werner Abelshauser, "Neuer Most in alten Schläuchen? Vorindustrielle Traditionen deutscher Wirtschaftsordnung im Vergleich mit England," in Dietmar Petzina and Jürgen Reulecke (Eds.), *Bevölkerung, Wirtschaft, Gesellschaft seit der Industrialisierung* (Dortmund: Gesellschaft für Westfälische Wirtschaftsgeschichte, 1990), pp. 117–132. The same conclusions are drawn by Heinz-Gerhard Haupt (Ed.), *Das Ende der Zünfte. Ein europäischer Vergleich*, Kritische Studien zur Geschichtswissenschaft 151 (Göttingen: Vandenhoeck & Ruprecht, 2002).

51. See Hermann Levy, *Monopole, Kartelle und Trusts*, 2nd ed. (Jena: Fischer, 1927), p. 13.

52. 21, Jacob, c. 3, I (*Statutes* VII), pp. 255–256.

53. *Cobbett's Parliamentary History of England*, vol. II (London: Bagshaw, 1807), column 656.

54. James I, Proclamation of 12 August 1617, *State Papers Domestic*, vol. XCIII, Proc. Coll. No. 50 A.

55. See Levy, *Monopole*, pp. 95–193.

56. "An Harborowe for Faithfull and Trewe Subjectes (1559)," in George Orwell and Reginald Reynolds (Eds.), *British Pamphleteers, vol. I: From the Sixteenth Century to the French Revolution* (London: Wingate, 1948), p. 31.

57. See especially Barry E. Supple, *Commercial Crisis and Change in England 1600-1642: A Study in the Instability of a Mercantile Economy* (Cambridge, England: Cambridge University Press, 1959), ch. 10.

58. See Robert Ashton, "Charles I and the City," in Frederick Jack Fisher (Ed.), *Essays in the Economic and Social History of Tudor and Stuart England* (Cambridge, England: Cambridge University Press, 1961), pp. 138–163.

59. Karl Marx, "Das Kapital. Kritik der politischen Ökonomie," in *Marx Engels Werke*, vol. 23, p. 621.

60. Ernst Troeltsch, *Die Soziallehren der christlichen Kirchen und Gruppen*, 2nd reprint (Aalen: Scientia, 1965, pp. 561 and 579. (Original work published 1922)

61. "In behaglicher Ruhe richteten sich nun die besitzenden Klassen in Stadt und Land ein, immer weiter die Staatsgewalt plündernd, - um sich wohlhabender zu machen, bis endlich das preußische Königtum und der aufgeklärte Despotismus überhaupt mit seinen Beamten Wandel schaffte." Gustav Schmoller, *Über einige Grundfragen der Socialpolitik und der Volkswirtschaftslehre* (Leipzig: Duncker & Humblot, 1898), p. 148.

62. Inaugural address at the constituent assembly of the Verein für Socialpolitik, 6 Oktober 1872, in Ständiger Ausschuß des Vereins (Ed.), *Verhandlungen der Eisenacher Versammlung zur Besprechung der sozialen Frage* (Leipzig: Duncker & Humblot, 1873), pp. 3–4.

63. Hermann Conrad und Gerd Kleinheyer (Eds.), *Wissenschaftliche Abhandlungen der Arbeitsgemeinschaft für Forschung des Landes Nordrhein-Westfalen: vol. 10. Vorträge über Recht und Staat von Carl Gottfried Svarez (1746–1798)* (Cologne: Westdeutscher Verlag, 1960), p. 89.

64. See Alexander Gerschenkron, "Economic backwardness in historical perspective," in Bert F. Hoselitz (Ed.), *The Progress of Underdeveloped Areas* (Chicago: University Press, 1952), pp. 3–29.

65. Albert Schäffle, "Vergangenheit und Zukunft der deutschen Gemeinde," in idem, *Gesammelte Aufsätze*, vol. 1 (Tübingen: Laupp'sche Buchhandlung, 1885), p. 50.

66. Albert Schäffle, "Abbruch und Neubau der Zunft," in *Gesammelte Aufsätze*, vol. 1, pp. 37–38.

67. Schmoller, *Grundfragen*, p. 69.

68. See Mihaïl Manoïlesco, *Le siècle du corporatisme. Docrine du corporatisme integral et pur* (Paris: Alcan, 1936), p. 7. (Original work published 1934)

69. See Maurizio Vaudagna, *Corporativismo e New Deal* (Turin: Rosenberg & Sellier, 1981).

70. Andrew Shonfield, *Modern Capitalism: The Changing Balance of Public and Private Power* (Oxford, England: Oxford University Press, 1965).

71. The title of the German edition (Cologne: Kiepenheuer & Witsch, 1974), with an introduction by Karl Schiller.

72. *The Review of Politics*, 36/1 (1974), 85–131.

73. W. Abelshauser, "Ansätze 'korporativer Marktwirtschaft' in der Korea-Krise der frühen fünfziger Jahre" (with documents), *Vierteljahrshefte für Zeitgeschichte 30* (1982), 715–756.

74. See Gerald D. Feldman, "Der deutsche organisierte Kapitalismus während der Kriegs- und Inflationsjahre 1914–1923," in Heinrich A. Winkler (Ed.), *Organisierter Kapitalismus* (Göttingen:Vandenhoeck & Ruprecht, 1974), pp. 150–171; idem (with Irmgard Steinisch), *Industrie und Gewerkschaften 1918–1924* (Stuttgart: Deutsche Verlagsanstalt, 1985); Charles S. Maier, *Recasting Bourgeois Europe* (Princeton, NJ: Princeton University Press, 1975).

75. P. Schmitter, "Modes of interest intermediation and models of societal change in Western Europe," *Comparative Political Studies*, 10/1 (1977), 11–12.

76. See Abelshauser, "Post-liberal Nation".

77. See Abelshauser, "Staat".

78. See Wolfram Fischer, *Unternehmerschaft, Selbstverwaltung und Staat* (Berlin: Duncker & Humblot, 1964), p. 74.

79. *Kreuzzeitung* (Berlin), 14 November 1880, p. 3.

80. Aufruf der Versammlung sämtlicher Berliner Innungs-Verbände am 10. Februar 1869, Zentrales Staatsarchiv Merseburg (ZStAM), Rep. 120 BB, VIa, 1.1.

81. Gesetz, betr. die Abänderung der Gewerbeordnung vom 26. Juli 1897, RGBl., p. 663. Guilds had to be established if desired by a majority of the people concerned.

82. See Hartmut Kaelble, *Industrielle Interessenpolitik in der Wilhelminischen Gesellschaft. Centralverband Deutscher Industrieller 1895 bis 1914* (Berlin: Walter de Gruyter & Co., 1967), p. 185; Siegfried Mielke, *Der Hansa-Bund für Gewerbe, Handel und Industrie 1909 bis 1914* (Göttingen: Vandenhoeck & Ruprecht, 1976), pp. 48, 81.

83. "Ohne Mitglied einer berechtigten Korporation zu sein … ist der Einzelne ohne Standesehre, durch seine Isolierung auf die selbstsüchtige Seite des Gewerbes reduziert, seine Subsistenz und Genuß nichts Stehendes." Georg Wilhelm Friedrich Hegel, *Sämtliche Werke: vol. 7. Grundlinien der Philosophie des Rechts*, 2nd ed. (Leipzig: Eckardt, 1938), § 253. The translations of Hegel in the present book draw on, but do not adopt verbatim, the version in *Hegel's Philosophy of Right*, translated with notes by T.M. Knox (Oxford, England: Clarendon Press, 1952).

84. "die Besorgung des besonderen Interesses als eines Gemeinsamen." Ibid., § 188.

85. "die höhere Aufsicht des Staates, … weil sie sonst verknöchern, sich in sich verhausen und zu einem elenden Zunftwesen herabsinken würde." Ibid., § 255.

86. "gesetzlich gemachte Bestimmungen, die in der Natur der Besonderheit eines wesentlichen Zweiges der Gesellschaft selbst liegen." Ibid., § 252.

87. "Wenn die Abgeordneten als Repräsentanten betrachtet werden, so hat dies einen organisch vernünftigen Sinn nur dann, daß sie nicht Repräsentanten als von Einzelnen, von einer Menge seien, sondern Repräsentanten einer der wesentlichen Sphären der Gesellschaft, Repräsentanten ihrer großen Interessen. Das Repräsentieren hat damit auch nicht mehr die Bedeutung, daß Einer an der Stelle eines Anderen sei, sondern das Interesse selbst ist in seinen Repräsentanten wirklich gegenwärtig," Ibid., § 311.

88. Hans Rothfels, *Theodor Lohmann und die Kampfjahre der staatlichen Sozialpolitik* (Berlin: Mittler, 1927), pp. 63–64.

89. Bismarck in the inaugural meeting of the Prussian Economic Council, 27 January 1881, ZStAM, Rep. 151 I C.

90. ZStAM, Rep. 120 A I 1, No. 81.

91. The people elected by the chambers and corporations for presentation were classified as "protectionists" and "free traders" and characterized by their attitude toward "national economic policy" before they were presented to Bismarck for selection. ZStAM, 2.2.1 Nr. 27681.

92. p. 14.

93. *Berliner politische Nachrichten*, 25 January 1884, p. 1.

94. Letter of the Minister for Trade and Industry to the Regional President in Münster, 7 January 1886, ZStAM, Rep. 151 I C, No. 9348.

95. Annual report for 1888 by the chamber of industry for the governmental district of Merseburg, Halle on the Saale River, ZStAM, Rep. 120 BB VIa, vol. 3. This appraisal was widely shared in connection with the economic conferences, whose raison d'être was increasingly doubted. See also the *Münsterischer Anzeiger*, 8 February 1891.

96. This was the demand from the protectionist Osnabrück chamber of commerce, whose plenary session of 30 October 1882 supported Bismarck's corporatism with a resolution on the reorganization of the representation of economic interests; ZStAM, Rep. 120 BB VIa 1.1.

97. The concept of cartels at the end of the nineteenth and beginning of the twentieth centuries is discussed, for example, in Friedrich Kleinwächter, "Kartelle," *Handwörterbuch der Staatswissenschaften*, 3rd ed. vol. 5 (Jena: Gustav Fischer, 1903), p. 792; Albert Schäffle, "Zum Kartellwesen und zur Kartellpolitik," *Zeitschrift für die gesamte Staatswissenschaft*, 54 (1898), 467–528, 647–719; Robert Liefmann, *Kartelle und Trusts*, 2nd ed. (Stuttgart: E.H. Moritz, 1909); with a bibliography on the issue of cartels: Hans-Heinrich Barnikel (Ed.), *Wege der Forschung, vol. 174. Bibliographie zum Kartellproblem: Theorie und Praxis der Kartelle* (Darmstadt: Wissenschaftliche Buchgesellschaft, 1972).

98. Adam Smith, *An Inquiry into the Nature and Causes of the Wealth of Nations* (2nd ed. from the 11th London ed.), vol. 1 (Hartford: Oliver D. Cooke, 1811), p. 92 (Original work published 1776); Gustav Schmoller, "Das Verhältnis der Kartelle zum Staat," in Verein für Socialpolitik (Ed.), *Verhandlungen des Vereins für Socialpolitik, Mannheim, 27–28 September 1905*, Schriften des Vereins für Socialpolitik, vol. 116 (Leipzig: Duncker & Humblot, 1906), p. 254.

99. Ibid., p. 248.

100. Werner Sombart, *Das Wirtschaftsleben im Zeitalter des Hochkapitalismus*, 2nd half volume, 4th ed. (Berlin: Duncker & Humblot, 1955), p. 696.

101. *Die Kartelle* (Innsbruck: Wagner, 1883), p. 216.

102. Max Weber, *Economy and Society: An Interpretive Outline of Sociology,* 2 vols., ed. by G. Roth and C. Wittich, trans. E. Fischoff, H. Gerth, A.M. Henderson, F. Kolegor, C. Wright Mills, T. Parsons, M. Eheinstein, G. Roth, E. Shils, and C. Wittich (Berkeley: University of California Press, 1978), p. 724. (Original work published 1922.)

103. Reichsamt des Innern (Ed.), *Kontradiktorische Verhandlungen über deutsche Kartelle. Die vom Reichsamt des Innern angestellten Erhebungen über das inländische Kartellwesen in Protokollen und Stenographischen Berichten*, vol. 1 (Berlin: Siemenroth, 1903), p. 259.

104. See Franz Böhm, "Das Reichsgericht und die Kartelle," *Ordo*, 1 (1948), p. 212.

105. See the contrasting view offered in Arno J. Mayer, *The Persistence of the Old Regime: Europe to the Great War* (New York: Pantheon, 1981).

106. See the debates in the executive committees of German unions (especially in August 1914 and from December 1916 through January 1917) in Klaus Schönhoven (Ed.), *Quellen zur Geschichte der deutschen Gewerkschaftsbewegung im 20. Jahrhundert: vol. 1. Die Gewerkschaften in Weltkrieg und Revolution 1914 bis 1919* (Cologne: Bund, 1985).

107. Heinrich Kaun, *Die Geschichte der Zentralarbeitsgemeinschaft der industriellen und gewerblichen Arbeitgeber Deutschlands* (Jena: Gustav Fischer, 1938), pp. 10–15.

108. See Dietmar Petzina, "Gewerkschaften und Monopolfrage vor und während der Weimarer Republik," *Archiv für Sozialgeschichte*, 20 (1980), 195–218.

109. See Ralph H. Bowen, *German Theories of the Corporative State* (New York and London: Mc Graw Hill, 1947), pp. 160–210.

110. Letter by Albert Vögler, General Director of the German-Luxembourg Mining and Smelting Works AG (Deutsch-Luxemburgische Bergwerks- und Hütten-AG) to Carl Gerwin, 24 June 1919, in Gerald D. Feldman and Heidrun Homburg, *Industrie und Inflation: Studien und Dokumente zur Politik der deutschen Unternehmer 1916–1923* (Hamburg: Hoffmann u. Campe, 1977), p. 217.

111. Minutes of a discussion in the Imperial Ministry of Economics, 15 May 1919, about the creation of a specific administrative union for the iron and steel industry. Ibid., pp. 215–216.

112. See Werner Abelshauser, "Verelendung der Handarbeit? Zur sozialen Lage der deutschen Arbeiter in der großen Inflation der frühen zwanziger Jahre," in Hans Mommsen and Winfried Schulze (Eds.), *Vom Elend der Handarbeit. Probleme historischer Unterschichtenforschung* (Stuttgart: Klett-Cotta, 1981), pp. 445–476.

113. Kaun, *Geschichte*, appendix II, p. 128.

114. Draft economic program by the RDI, Bundesarchiv (National Archive), Silverberg Estate, No. 313, reprinted in Feldman and Homburg, *Industrie*, pp. 324–327.

115. Letter by Ministerial Council Franz Kempner to Undersecretary Eduard Hamm, Reich Chancellery, 6 January 1923, BA, R 431/1133, p. 170.

116. Minutes of the second meeting of the RDI's special economic program committee, 9 August 1922, Bundesarchiv (National Archive), Silverberg Estate, No. 312, reprinted in Feldman and Homburg, *Industrie*, p. 340.

117. *Jahrbuch 1928 des Allgemeinen Deutschen Gewerkschaftsbunds* [ADGB] (Berlin: Verlagsgesellschaft des ADGB, 1929), p. 34.

118. Ludwig Preller, *Sozialpolitik in der Weimarer Republik* (Stuttgart: Franz Mittelbach, 1949), p. 509.

119. Paul Silverberg, "Das deutsche industrielle Unternehmertum in der Nachkriegszeit," in *Veröffentlichungen des RDI*, vol. 32 (Berlin: RDI, 1926), pp. 55–65.

120. Ibid., p. 65.

121. See Gerald D. Feldman, *Iron and Steel in the German Inflation, 1916–23* (Princeton, NJ: Princeton University Press, 1977), p. 465, and Bernd Weisbrod, *Schwerindustrie in der Weimarer Republik* (Wuppertal: Hammer, 1978), pp. 255–272.

122. See, for example, Vaudagna, *Corporativismo*, and Keith Middlemas, *Politics in Industrial Society: The Experience of the British System since 1911* (London: André Deutsch, 1979).

123. *Gewerkschafts-Zeitung* (Berlin), 1930, p. 308.

124. See the minutes of a discussion between RDI's executive committee and VDA's managing board on 3 June 1930, Bundesarchiv (National Archive), Silverberg Estate, No. 457, in Ilse Maurer and Udo Wengst (Eds.), with an introduction by Gerhard Schulz, *Politik und Wirtschaft in der Krise 1930–1932, Quellen zur Ära Brüning*, Part 1 (Düsseldorf: Droste, 1980), pp. 190–191; Minutes of the session of the Federal Committee of the ADGB on 14–15 December 1930, in ibid., p. 495.

125. Ibid., p. 191.

126. *Gewerkschafts-Zeitung* (Berlin), 1930, p. 380.

127. Draft statement of President von Hindenburg about the negotiations between entrepreneurs and unions, BA, R 43/I/1157, in Maurer and Wengst, *Politik und Wirtschaft*, Part 1, pp. 198–199.

128. Joint discussion on 3 June 1930, BA, Nl Silverberg, No. 457, ibid., pp. 190–191.

129. See the study by Dieter Hertz-Eichenrode, *Wirtschaftskrise und Arbeitsbeschaffung. Konjunkturpolitik 1925/26 und die Grundlagen der Krisenpolitik Brünings* (Frankfurt am Main and New York: Campus, 1982).

130. Minutes of the discussion on 3 June, Bundesarchiv (National Archive), Silverberg Estate, No. 457, in Maurer and Wengst, *Politik und Wirtschaft*, Part 1, p. 191.

131. See "Entwurf für eine gemeinsame Erklärung von Unternehmerverbänden und Gewerkschaften" and "Aufzeichnung Blanks über eine Mitteilung Kastls," both in Maurer and Wengst, *Politik und Wirtschaft*, Part 1, pp. 194–196.

132. See also Reinhard Neebe, "Konflikt und Kooperation 1930–1933: Anmerkungen zum Verhältnis von Kapital und Arbeit in der Weltwirtschaftskrise," in W. Abelshauser (Ed.), *Die Weimarer Republik als Wohlfahrtsstaat. Zum Verhältnis von Wirtschafts- und Sozialpolitik in der Industriegesellschaft, Vierteljahresschrift für Sozial- und Wirtschaftsgeschichte,* (Supplement 81) (Stuttgart: Steiner, 1987), pp. 226–238.

133. See Udo Wengst, "Unternehmerverbände und Gewerkschaften in Deutschland im Jahre 1930," *Vierteljahrshefte für Zeitgeschichte* 25 (1977), p. 102.

134. That doctrine was based on two social encyclicals, the Encyclica Rerum Novarum (On the Question of the Workers, issued by Pope Leo XIII on 15 May 1891) and Quadragesimo Anno (with which Pope Pius XI intended to endorse the Rerum Novarum on 31 May 1931). See *On the Conditions of the Workers, Leo XIII, and Forty Years After, On Reconstruction of Social Order, Pius XI,* Latin Text with English Translation, approved by the Holy See (New York and Boston: The Catholic University of America Press, 1943).

135. Communicated at the meeting of the Federal Committee of the ADGB, 14–15 December 1930, in Maurer and Wengst, *Politik und Wirtschaft,* Part 1, pp. 496–498.

136. Ibid., p. 497.

137. Ibid., p. 505.

138. Minutes of the meeting of the ADGB managing board, in Maurer and Wengst, *Politik und Wirtschaft,* Part 1, p. 524.

139. An anticyclical approach to providing jobs by creating credit, conceived by the union representatives Vladimir Voytinski, Fritz Tarnow, and Fritz Baade (the VTB plan), was coolly received even in their own ADGB ranks and was unconditionally rejected by the SPD faction in the Reichstag.

140. Translation of an excerpt from the report of the Central Committee of the Provisional National Economic Council, 12 March 1932, in Maurer and Wengst, *Politik und Wirtschaft,* Part 2, p. 1321.

141. Ibid., p. 1325.

142. Maier, *Recasting,* p. 592.

143. See Werner Abelshauser, *Deutsche Wirtschaftsgeschichte seit 1945* (Munich: C.H. Beck, 2004), pp. 409–420.

III. The German Production Regime

Notes for this section begin on page 119.

1. The Production Regime of the Coordinated Market Economy

Institutional Prerequisites of Diversified Quality Production

Identifying the hallmarks of any country's production regime requires a high degree of abstract thinking and ideal-type conceptualization. This is especially true of Germany, however, where the economy has developed numerous important interlocking regional systems that constitute integrated industrial units, each having its own specializations and comparative institutional advantages. Most of these clusters of economically interrelated companies have preserved their interlocking character to this day, examples being the Rhine-Main area, North and East Württemberg, the sites of heavy industry and New Industries along both banks of the Rhine River, East Westphalia-Lippe, Saxony, the Hanseatic cities, the Munich area, and the industrial region of central Germany between Hanover, Magdeburg, and Halle. They are presently the backbone of Germany's export business not only because they accumulated an attractive industrial culture throughout the twentieth century but also because their transaction costs are significantly lower than those of their German and international rivals as a result of a long-standing, institutional setting that builds trust. These regions thus enjoy decisive advantages over others. Some of the classical industrial regions, such as the Ruhr District, changed their nature completely during the twentieth century; others, such as Greater Berlin, largely lost the leading position they used to have and have not fully regained it since 1945. Still others, such as the Saar, Silesia, and many similar traditional European homes of heavy industry, have not yet developed a new, competitive profile.

It would make little sense to compare the production regimes of individual sites without placing them in a specific context. The choice of the product market that should serve as the reference point is obviously decisive if the attributes and performance of a site are to be judged. Consequently, the question about a production regime's strengths and weaknesses may have no single answer. On the supply side, it depends on regional criteria; on the demand side, on product-specific criteria. Nevertheless, it may be useful to begin with an ideal-type description of the nationwide social system of production in order then to categorize the way in which individual companies, sectors, and markets of a country's economy are organized and how they came about. After all, most components of sectorial production regimes coalesced at the level of the nation-state. There, their effect continues to develop regardless of trends toward "Europeanization" through the legal system of the European Union and practices growing out of increasingly transnational economic activity.

The description of what the German production regime is capable of has recently come mainly from observers outside Germany. They see it as nothing more and nothing less than the engrained culture of the market economy in Germany. It is noted for its long-term corporate financing and unrestricted intrasectorial technology transfer in a multifaceted system of vocational education and training that companies help to structure, from apprenticeship to colleges of applied sciences. Another feature is the inter- and intracompany cooperation between the industrial partners. Not infrequently, leading economists outside Germany have lately given German institutions high marks for efficiency, an appraisal that often surprises German onlookers, who tend toward self-criticism. According to American international trade expert Michael Porter,[1] the great comparative advantage of the German export sector and, hence, the key reason behind its enduring success lies hidden in the German model of a market economy. Comparing the German and American economic systems directly, the British economic researcher David Soskice[2] sees what he calls the "business-coordinated market economy" as an abidingly successful social system of production, particularly under the conditions of globalization. The French top manager and best-selling author Michel Albert even advises the French to adopt what he calls "Rhine capitalism" because it is socially and economically superior to the Anglo-Saxon model.[3]

To all these foreign observers, the adjective "social" in the social market economy has two meanings: social partnership and entrepreneurial coordination. Because both core elements of German corporate culture are based on sociability (trustful cooperation in the economic process), Francis Fukuyama sees that foundation as a prerequisite for a structurally low level of economic transaction costs and thus for competitiveness on the world market. He therefore underscores the role of trust and societal virtues as sources of prosperity in world society.[4] In his opinion, cultural factors of this kind are determining the competitiveness of global economic actors more and more. Precisely because the framework of Germany's institutions is rooted in history, Fukuyama considers the country to be well equipped for the market competition between cultures, especially economic cultures, in the twenty-first century.

The basis for these and similar judgments about the overall macroeconomic strengths and weaknesses of the manner in which an economy is organized, specifically its production regime, is the comparison with other social systems of production—particularly those that may also serve as ideal types and that compete against Germany's system. For Germany, the chief reference point is the production regime of the United States of America, which the conditions of globalization and the rapid rise of the knowledge society have put well on the way to setting the worldwide standards for successful economic organization in the twenty-first century.[5] Which of these systems will cope best with the challenges of the future is a question no longer only of academic interest. It has assumed forms of a fierce cultural struggle in German economic life.

The particulars of the German and American production regimes show up clearly when the two are compared (see Table 2). The American production regime is diametrically opposed to the German in nearly every respect and can be described in ideal-type terms as a liberal market economy based on free competition and oriented to short-term return. Its institutional advantages therefore exist predominantly on product markets shaped by radical innovations and the use of new technologies. Long-range comparison of the two production regimes shows that they had more in common with each other when they emerged at the end of the nineteenth century than now, one hundred years later (see Table 3). This initial likeness is not surprising, for they were responding to similar challenges posed by the onset of market internationalization and industry's intensifying reliance on science. The efficiency of the German and American production regimes must be measured in terms of how they cope with economic difficulties that, although not altogether new, quickly become telling under those conditions. During the long process of industrialization, for example, the ability to deal productively with the property-rights paradigm set the pace and quality of economic development. In the postindustrial era, however, the agency problem and the control of transaction costs increasingly determine the success of nonmaterial production.

Of course, the characteristic differences marking the divergence of the two systems have always been unmistakable and are still apparent today. They stem in great part from the fact that the new institutions at the end of the nineteenth century resorted to the societal, economic, and legal patterns of thought that were already familiar, the purpose being to minimize the costs of gaining acceptance. Beholden to Anglo-Saxon common law, the organizational principles of the American economy followed the paradigm of competition. In Germany, the corporatist and cooperative tradition prevailed, a paradigm that had shaped industrial development in the German territories. Other points of divergence in the production regimes of the United States and Germany resulted from fundamental differences in market morphology, not least that of the labor markets. Economic historians writing after 1945 have drawn profound conclusions from this contrast between the organizational principles of the two national economies, seeing it as a cause of aberrations that ultimately led to the catastrophe of the Third Reich in Germany.

Table 2. Divergence of Production Regimes in the Late Nineteenth Century

Germany	United States
Labor market, qualification, and participation of employees	
Long-term employment	Short-term employment
Deregulated labor markets	Deregulated labor markets
Industry- and company-specific vocational training	General qualifications outside vocational training
Principal-Agent problem	Principal-Agent problem
Finance system and corporate governance	
High-risk finance	High-risk finance
Long-term modes of financing, weak capital markets	Short-term modes of financing, highly liquid capital markets
Strong links between bank and firm	Highly liquid equities
"Stakeholder value"	"Stakeholder value"
Intercompany system	
Vertical and horizontal concentration	Vertical and horizontal concentration
Long-term interlocking capital relations, no "hostile" acquisitions	Strong merger and acquisition activities
Industrial districts ("clusters"), flexible production	Industrial districts ("clusters"), flexible production
Corporatist interest policy (strong business associations)	Pluralist interest policy (weak business associations)
Open transfer of technology (vocational training based on industry standard)	Competition in technology
Tolerance of collective action (cartels)	Antitrust legislation

Source: © Werner Abelshauser

Table 3. Divergence of Production Regimes in the Late Twentieth Century

Germany	United States
Ideal types	
Business-coordinated market economy	Liberal market economy
Capacity to innovate	
Quality production with established technology	Radical innovations with new technology
Entrepreneurial behavior	
Long-term Highly cooperative	Short-term Highly contentious
Labor market, qualification, and participation of employees	
Highly qualified, long-term employment	Narrowly defined and specific; short-term employment
Institutionalized bargaining	Deregulated labor markets
Industry- and company-specific vocational training	General qualifications outside vocational training
Codetermination	Principal-Agent problem
Financing and corporate governance	
Strong links between bank and firm	Highly liquid equities
Long-term modes of finance	Short-term modes of finance, high-risk finance
Weak capital markets	Highly liquid capital markets
"Stakeholder value"	"Shareholder value"
Intercompany system	
Long-term "interlocking" capital relations, no "hostile" acquisitions	Strong merger and acquisition activities
Diversified quality production in established regional clusters of industries	Mass standardized production (with exceptions in the "new economy")
Corporatist interest policy (strong business associations)	Pluralist interest policy (weak business associations)
Open transfer of technology (vocational training based on industry standard)	Competition in technology
Tolerance of various forms of collective action	Antitrust legislation

Source: © Werner Abelshauser

In actuality, however, the social systems of production in the United States and Germany differ less in function than in appearance. The numerous paradoxes of globalization weighed on both countries, particularly since they were the pioneers in the first phase of the process. For example, a certain amount of protectionism was needed wherever the stability of business and society was threatened by the ruinous and self-destructive impacts that the mighty and unprecedented dynamics of foreign trade had on the internal structure of the economy. Strengthening the nation-state was another essential ingredient in the functioning of the world markets and their power to expand. Only global players with indisputable authority could negotiate the rules of transnational interactions and establish the commensurate "infrastructure," including the gold standard as the international medium of finance. And given the harsher competitive conditions and long-term planning horizons for new investment, it seemed more necessary than ever to stabilize the national markets by controlling them through whatever methods were available.

Outwardly, the new institutional mold remained untouched by such calculations. All in all, it had a different end to serve. The more fundamental the upheaval was in the development of the production regime and its components, the more pressing it became to solve the problem of acceptance. If the cardinal institutional purpose of the economy was to create a stable order for reducing the uncertainty of human interactions—and hence also the costs of overcoming it[6]—then it was crucial for new institutions to be introduced in familiar guises. It was the only way to compensate for the lack of the trust and confidence that they had had no time to inspire and accumulate. Even cartels, an innovation of the coordinated market economy of the late nineteenth century, used this method. To contemporaries, this organizational approach to economic activity was a way of modifying the idea of the cooperative and applying it to modern industrial production. One question is the extent to which such historical analogies and memories facilitated institutional change by helping undercut the resistance to modernization that openly surfaced in the controversy surrounding the industrial state at the turn of the twentieth century.[7]

The attempt to imbue the new production regime with ideological and moral legitimacy also enhanced its debut. For instance, the representatives of the German historical school of political economics in the Association for Social Policy never tired of deriving from their own Prusso-German tradition a higher ethical standard for economic activity than seemed possible from Anglo-Saxon economic history. The British economy, which was still the leader of world economic development, therefore no longer served as something to emulate but rather as a contrasting institutional model. The aim was to overtake it instead of catch up to what was recognized as its "historically" obsolete state of development, which was reflected in the production regime.

The debate about the industrial state has hitherto been regarded primarily in terms of its politically mobilizing and socially polarizing sway on interest intermediation in the German empire. Upon closer consideration, however, it also reveals the basic currents that effected the institutional break with liberal conventions—both industrial and agrarian—and the adoption of the new course, the coordinated market economy. The radical shift in the production regime also indicates a fundamental change in society's production potential. It grew out of key changes in society's state of knowledge and called for a new organizational architecture realizing this new dimension of economic activity. The revolutionary nature of these economic possibilities thus lies not only in the close link between science and technology in the production process. It lies above all in the recognition that the institutional context required reorganization if these reserves of productivity were to be mobilized on the markets, in companies, and in economic policy.[8]

Coordinated Market Economy

Toward the end of the nineteenth century, a new and stable social system of production had developed in Germany. Its basic principle was not competition but rather cooperation between the economic actors. The organization of production reflected the self-governance and overriding collaboration that characterized the equally new system in which it was embedded, the corporatist interest intermediation that had developed during the 1880s. The typical feature thereof was a dual organizational structure at the top level of joint-stock corporations. In this arrangement, which came about through the 1884 reform of corporate law, the operational control of enterprises was assigned to a managing board, whereas basic decisions and important personnel issues became the responsibility of a supervisory board. The supervisory board's composition enabled large companies to build communications networks for directing information from significant areas of the economy into the proper channels. There, it improved the basis for business decisions and accrued trust that helps keep the transaction costs low within the various economic sectors.

To this day, appointing bank representatives to supervisory boards facilitates their control of the businesses whose long-term financing they arrange as the company bank or member of a banking consortium. Joint-stock corporations raise their venture capital on the stock exchange, but there, too, the banks do the underwriting, exercise proxy voting rights for most of the shareholders, and thereby contribute to the long-term stability of finance relations. Investors, including small shareholders, still do not embrace the principle of shareholder value but rather behave like stakeholders, who forego short-term gains in order to optimize their long-term profit by adding to the resources and financial health of "their" company. Accordingly, the German production regime goes a long way to accommodating a long-term and sustainable business perspective.

This regime's other components, such as the intercompany system (a cooperative relationship that companies in an industry form among themselves through such structures as associations, shared research facilities, educational institutions, export cartels, and sales syndicates), industrial relations, and the training system, function in a similar manner. Cooperation comes before competition, a principle that ensures a high degree of stable quality production through a dual system in which schools and companies organize training in cooperation with associations and in partnership with unions. Training content is oriented to the technological state of the art in each sector.

The discrete components of the social system of production mesh so tightly that it would be difficult to replace any one of them with an alien component as though it were a module.[9] The dual organization of vocational training plays an influential role. The business community joins the public sector in investing considerable sums in a system that allows them (together with the unions) to determine much of what must be taught and to equip themselves to meet the technological requirements of their sector. This approach, however, demands long-term modes of finance because the returns on these investments in human capital do not come in for a long time. A coordinated wage policy is essential in order to minimize the danger of labor poaching. Cooperative labor relations are pivotal to ensuring the loyalty of a highly qualified and stable core workforce. Lastly, companies must closely cooperate on technology transfer and standardization in order to develop universally recognized standards on which to base training and vocational testing. Long-term modes of financing, in turn, call for certain forms of corporate governance and strong associations that can give creditors the imperative guarantee of information flow. This reasoning could easily be extended to each and every subsystem of the German production regime.

All in all, the German model of a coordinated market economy can be understood as a production regime based on long-term perspective and cooperation. Its comparative institutional advantages play out predominantly in product markets for the exchange of diversified quality production that uses highly developed, applied technologies and whose strength is in long-term customer relations.[10] This description delineates something beyond industrial customization relying on production methods of the traditional crafts and on collective sorts of cooperation that proved resistant to the Taylorist division of work introduced toward the end of the nineteenth century. What arose in Germany from the 1880s on corresponded instead to the technological state of the art practiced above all by New Industries, which were in the ascendant at that time. The innovative core of diversified quality production as it emerged in late nineteenth-century machine manufacturing, the electronics industry, and major chemical plants was the nonmaterial value creation arising from the new types of symbiotic relations between business and science in those sectors. It was a production process for manufacturing commodities without the direct input of goods or services in the conventional sense. Value creation came less from the conversion of material, as in classical Old Industry, than from integrated knowledge about many things, including market needs, solutions to problems through research and development, manufacturing processes, applications and processing possibilities, and integrated services that facilitate timely production, delivery, financing, and guaranteed quality.

Before World War I, the institutional prerequisites for this kind of nonmaterial production existed in only a few European countries and the United States. In the United States, the capacity for diversified quality work was not based on universally accepted, socially embedded rules or solid institutions such as associations or formal legal norms. It remained the achievement of individual major companies, which in this respect resembled islands in a sea of conventional and quite simple production patterns.[11] In Germany, however, the social system of the coordinated market economy broadly supported diversified quality work by, for example, opening long-term horizons for venturesome business strategies and decisions, ensuring a superior standard of quality and a motivated workforce, and affording the collective inputs from basic research that were crucial to this production pattern. The high density and integration of the institutional framework and the capacity for intraindustry sociability—the basis for building trust—are resources that have grown over long periods and owe their existence to the peculiarities of German industrial development. The same is true for the agglomerations of regional clusters whose multifarious, close, and steady supply relations are some of the economic synergies distinguishing many of the "industrial districts" (Alfred Marshall) that have evolved in Germany. They enable Germany's export business to offer materially and temporally flexible, reasonably priced products for the world market.

Although diversified quality work took place primarily in the major enterprises of New Industries, it depended—as it always has and still does—on a well-coordinated substructure of small and medium-size plants that included the craft businesses of the sectors involved. After a long phase with no privileges toward the end of the nineteenth century, the crafts regained rights of incorporation and furnished most of industry's skilled labor until well into the 1930s. The crafts remained the leading wellspring of highly skilled industrial labor even after the Reich Education Act of 1938 introduced industrial vocational training in all sectors of the economy. Nevertheless, it would be wrong to classify the new production pattern as craft-based. Diversified quality work was not confined to single-unit production, as was usually the case in machine manufacturing, nor did the production methods used have much in common with practices in the traditional crafts.

The German production regime thus not only possessed the material and institutional wherewithal for manufacturing specialized goods with general means of production. In keeping with the paradigm of mass production, it was also able to supply standardized goods with specialized means of production. On markets open to the sale of vast quantities of quality goods, the German production regime made it possible to compete successfully also with large lot sizes of customized quality products, as the international success of the chemical industry proved. There were two reasons why German industry before World War I showed little inclination to follow the American example of standardized mass manufacturing. First, Germany had its own sophisticated and flexible production pattern. What is more, that pattern was successful because it enjoyed great comparative cost advantages on the markets of paramount importance to German industry. Second, neither domestic nor foreign demand provided a powerful incentive to adopt complementary batch production, a condition exacerbated between the two world wars because of Germany's weak growth and the crisis of the globalization process. Despite these hostile conditions, the American challenge did have repercussions on the German production regime. Although the Fordist alternative did not become established as a second production method in Germany until the 1930s, the country experienced four decades of dualism between diversified quality work and standardized mass production. The rise, fall, and absorption of the "American" production method in Germany are instructive examples of the longevity and resilience that the production regime of the coordinated market economy has always demonstrated vis-à-vis external challenges.

2. The American Challenge

The Fordist Alternative

When Henry Ford's first Model T rolled off the assembly line in Highland Park, Michigan, in 1913, it was not the upbeat to but rather the climax of decades of development in a production pattern that adapted ever better to the conditions of the American markets as time passed. During the nineteenth century, a gigantic, rapidly integrating domestic market and a critical scarcity of qualified labor pushed many economic sectors into the hands of monopoly-like trusts, the only sources of capital for systematically applying new scientifically grounded manufacturing methods. They were based on the mass production of standardized models with the aid of specialized machines and facilities, each for a single piece of the whole assembly. The idea was to manufacture standardized goods in batches of unprecedented size. Offered at cutthroat prices made possible by large economies of scale, standardized consumer and production goods ranging from wristwatches to combine harvesters increasingly conquered the American market. What Ford stressed about these practices, which had been entrenched for a long time by the eve of World War I, was the systematic nature of his approach. Not only did it enable him to synchronize the discrete steps in the mechanical production process so precisely that traditional craft skills became dispensable, it went far beyond the organization of the production process. His concept reflected a recognition of the fact that mass production is inconceivable without mass consumption and that the manufacturer's own pricing and high-wage policy therefore abetted the spread of such consumption. Moreover, Ford's approach systematically capitalized on enormous productivity reserves thanks to the division of labor, which Frederick W. Taylor had perfected in his *Principles of Scientific Management*.[12] The Taylorist plant was a "paradise of the unskilled" but a tragedy for the skilled worker.[13] Yet it was precisely this difference that made Taylor's teachings so attractive for mass manufacturing in the United States. By 1917, when the United States and its superiority in mass-produced weapons and equipment had decided the war of attrition in Flanders in favor of the Entente, the merits of Fordist production methods had sunk in among Europeans as well.

Although none of the incentives of the American production pattern were effective in Europe, Germany, of all countries, was among those that succumbed early to the fascination of Fordism. In the 1920s German business leaders went on pilgrimages to the United States in order to probe the secret of their own economic future at the holy sites of capitalism. To many of them, those shrines were the new Ford factories in Highland Park and River Rouge, Michigan. Henry Ford's autobiography, *My Life and Work*, which was published in German in late 1923, was a best-seller from the outset. Appearing just as the business community was reorienting itself to the stabilization of Germany's currency and economy, the book prompted the first of many exploratory missions to Detroit, Michigan, by numerous engineers, unionists, managers, and journalists. Once back in Germany, nearly all these visitors to Detroit were firmly convinced of the revolutionary impacts of the new production methods. As early as 1925, the lectures on Fordism given by the social scientist Friedrich von Gottl-Ottlilienfeld were among the premier events at Humboldt University in Berlin. The idea that it was time to pave the way for a new age of mass production was projected mostly onto the automotive industry. Fordism developed into a strong, motivating force behind the many efforts to concentrate Germany's production capacity for passenger vehicles on a small number of major companies in order to achieve high economies of scale. Since the stabilization of the currency, large German banks, especially Deutsche Bank, had toyed with the idea of amalgamating the key, though only medium-size, German automotive manufacturers such as Daimler, Benz, Opel, and BMW into a large automobile group capable of meeting the Fordist challenge. Daimler and Benz merged in the years 1924 through 1926. All further attempts, however, foundered on adverse economic conditions and ended abruptly when Adam Opel AG in Rüsselsheim was sold to General Motors at a huge profit in early 1929. The transaction foreclosed any further discussion of setting up a German automotive group at the time. Indeed, the creeping crisis in the German automotive industry then became obvious. It henceforth became impossible to bridge the discrepancy between a serious debate about technological and theoretical aspects of Fordism and the miserable economic condition of the markets for mass-produced goods, particularly for cars. The Great Depression of the early 1930s destroyed the economic foundations of mass production, and not only in Germany. By the will of Hitler's government, however, the automotive industry was precisely what would end up helping to overcome the crisis. In doing so, that sector finally caught up with developments in the Fordist method of production. Competing head-to-head in the race to rearm, that sector gave rise to one of the most original creations of Fordism in Europe, the Volkswagen (VW) factory.

Fordist Strategic Approaches in the German Automotive Industry between the World Wars

Before 1933, the end of the Great Depression in Germany, the German automotive industry came nowhere near the leading role that its American model had in the industrial development of the United States during the Roaring Twenties. Not that Germany lacked the general microeconomic prerequisites for successfully introducing methods of Fordist mass production. Basically, the technical and organizational know-how existed, and there was keen interest in the new approaches to industrial relations. Mass production was recognized to be far superior to diversified quality work on markets for durable consumer goods because mass production's competitive prices and appeal to mass taste could serve whole strata of buyers who had not yet been reached.

The macroeconomic conditions, however, were not exactly conducive to an introduction of Fordist methods. Reconstruction of the German economy after World War I had suffered a grievous setback due to hyperinflation in 1923. The postwar dynamics of economic growth had slowed after currency stabilization, too, because of the Reichsbank's restrictive monetary policies, which kept interest rates high in order to attract foreign capital to Germany for financing reparations. Nor was foreign trade able to stoke the demand that would have been necessary to achieve economies of scale. Other hurdles arose, too. In the United States, part of Fordism's attraction stemmed from industry's constantly having to assimilate unseasoned labor into the production process. The German labor market of the 1920s and 1930s faced quite different problems. Endeavors to bring modern, efficient methods to industry—the rationalization movement—were aimed at improving the usefulness of the country's relatively large body of skilled labor, that is, at fully exploiting its productivity capacity to the benefit of the production process. The conditions on the labor market thus tended to impede the advent of Fordism in Germany. The final factor preventing the spread of mass production, specifically the "automobile society," was the weak demand that prevailed during the interwar years. Quite apart from the country's lack of transport infrastructure, broad segments of the population simply could not afford the maintenance, fuel, insurance, and taxes that a car entailed.

Continuous production and the assembly-line work that went with it therefore made only slow headway in the German automotive industry. Although Adam Opel AG started using assembly-line work as early as 1923, many German automobile factories did not follow suit until the Great Depression of the early 1930s.[14] Under these conditions, the productivity gap between the United States and Germany almost inevitably widened further. According to calculations by the National Association of the Automotive Industry in 1926,[15] the Ford Motor Company in Detroit produced one car for every 5.75 workers there. By contrast, the German company Horch needed more than 230 workers, and Daimler-Benz no fewer than 450, to produce one car in the same amount of time.

However, German automotive companies made rapid progress whenever they tried to catch up by applying Fordist methods to rationalize, or streamline, processes. By 1929, prices had fallen to half their 1924 levels. Output soared by more than 300 percent, and employment rose by about 50 percent. But even the "most American" German manufacturer, Adam Opel AG in Rüsselsheim, never came close to a level comparable to Detroit's. The continuous production that had been practiced at Opel since 1923 was still a far cry from the use made of the conveyor belt at Ford. In 1924 the assembly line at Opel was said to have been no longer than fifty yards. Until 1929 the production process was still spread across several nonadjacent plants, with the conveyor belt coming into use only for final assembly.[16] Opel trailed far behind the typical Fordist one-minute pace. In Rüsselsheim, cars left the assembly line only at a rate of one every 4.5 minutes, or 105 cars a day with a workforce of seven thousand people.

Nevertheless, the technical and organizational side of automotive production in the late 1920s was highly developed in Germany, too. According to statistics compiled by the Association of German Metalworkers, 7 of the 29 important automotive manufacturers (i.e., 24.2 percent, representing 2,467 employed people) had not renewed their capital stock; 4 (i.e., 13.8 percent, representing 12,119 employed people) had renewed part of it; and 18 (i.e., 62 percent, representing 30,902 employed people) had renewed all of it.[17]

Technical progress did not coincide with economic success, however. The collapse of the global economy in the early 1930s plunged the German automotive industry into a severe crisis. Numerous business failures and mergers eliminated most of the eighty-six automobile companies that had existed in the 1920s, leaving only a dozen that survived the Great Depression. In addition to Daimler-Benz, Opel, and the Cologne Ford factories founded in 1929, the market now had the Auto-Union AG, which had formed from the 1932 merger of four Saxon automotive manufacturers: the Zschopauer-Motoren-Werke, Horch, Wanderer, and Audi. This core group in the industry became a leading factor in Germany's comeback from the Depression, not least because it benefited in a special way from the National Socialist policy of resolutely promoting the motorization of German society and, later, the armed forces after 1933. The regime, in fact Hitler himself, urged the automotive industry to take on the Fordist challenge and jointly develop and produce a Volkswagen, a people's car, that would sustain mass motorization as Ford's Model T had done. Industry stubbornly resisted, so the government itself finally acted in 1938 by founding the VW factory, which in its last phase of expansion in the 1940s was to achieve a capacity of 1.5 million cars a year. Despite a shortage of foreign currency, the plant was equipped with highly specialized, single-purpose machines from the United States and was financed with the assets stolen from the unions by the regime. Work could not commence until 1940, however, and when it did, the factory focused solely on the production of military vehicles—for obvious reasons. Success measurable by international standards had to wait until well into the 1950s. As is shown seven pages below, the VW example thus also illustrates the idiosyncrasies of "West German Fordism" that resulted from the clash between "American" principles and the classical pattern of diversified quality production.[18]

Fordism during the War: The Krupp Case

One of the paradoxes of the German war economy is that it extended well beyond the efforts to arm the country in the first half of the 1940s; it laid the foundations for rapid reconstruction of the country's economy after 1945 as well. One of the cornerstones was the experience the arms industry had to acquire quickly in order to mass produce weapons, vehicles, and ammunition, a crash course for which the government paid dearly. Beset by military exigencies and facing the threat of defeat, German industry also liberated innovative forces that had been unable to flourish under the restrictive conditions of the Weimar Republic's economy in the 1920s and early 1930s. A particularly effective measure was the introduction of new, "American" management and manufacturing methods. At the outbreak of the war, the German arms industry was far outpaced by the Anglo-American capacity for mass production. By the autumn of 1941, though, Germany had considerably shortened the foe's lead in the rationalization of industrial processes and by late 1943 had pulled about even at the technological and organizational level.[19] Of course, the window of opportunity to overtake the enemy altogether was open only briefly. Lack of skilled labor and raw materials often thwarted commencement of serial production as of 1944.

One example of such failure was the tedious and ultimately abortive creation of a new, "fully automated" weapons factory by Fried. Krupp AG, the Bertha factory near Breslau.[20] This long-established company in Essen had successfully withdrawn from the arms industry in the 1920s and had shed its status as "old industry" by converting into a "department store of the peace industry."[21] Krupp had thus made a complete transition to the methods of diversified quality production, which had hitherto been confined to the manufacture of cannon. In the mid-1930s, however, the former arms corporation was confronted once more with the "venerable tradition of the house"[22] and saw itself compelled to forsake its new course and gradually return to accepting military contracts. With increasing frequency, the board of directors noted that the Krupp factory in Essen was prepared for the manufacture of quality armaments products but not for the mass production of weapons and equipment. The Ministry for Armaments and Munitions, headed by the engineer Dr. Fritz Todt, was not the only client pushing for a switch to the methods of

Fordist mass production; the company's civilian customers, too, such as the Reichsbahn (the German State Railroad), began submitting relatively large orders for series of products based on the same design. Krupp welcomed this development, but because of spatial constraints the company could not finish more than four or five heavy freight-train locomotives a week, let alone systematically switch over to mass production.

Krupp's abstinence in the processing of innovative raw materials and prototypes became a nuisance in other ways, too. More and more frequently, Krupp had to bend to the orders of the armaments authorities and share company secrets with potential competitors so that they could mass produce with the prototypes and process innovations developed in Essen. The Krupp method of casting and processing stainless steel, for example, had to be passed to two companies that matured to become potential rivals in the postwar period. Even before the arms boom, the factory in Essen had also come to know and appreciate other advantages of having its own manufacturing capacities for mass-produced goods. The process for innovating the new hard metal Widia (cemented composites of tungsten carbide-cobalt) never really took off until Krupp itself decided to find ways of using the tool-cutting metal and to set high quality standards that would underpin the international reputation and high market value of the brand.

As pressure during the war grew to tell competitors the secret of Widia's active agents in the interest of arming the country, the Krupp management formulated a new business policy of whose profound consequences the executive board was well aware. In addition to pursuing diversified quality production, the corporation would adopt Fordist standardized mass production of its own prototypes and innovations—not just as a way to cope with the immediate imperatives of arms production but also as a long-term postwar strategy. Serial production by Krupp was not to be an end in itself, however. Rather, it was intended to facilitate the logical continuation of the process for coming up with new kinds of steel and other inventions from the "main laboratory," the factory in Essen. This objective, which was not untypical for introducing new methods of mass production in the German economy, amounted to something like squaring the circle, especially in a war economy. Basically, it was not about standardized mass production but rather about standardized *quality* production. Weapons planners, from Hitler on down to the lower echelons of the Ministry of Armaments and Munitions, in effect got carried away with their dreams of what the German arms industry could do. It was enticing to envision how mass manufacture of the proverbially high quality of Krupp products would yield the ideal solution to many of the problems plaguing the German arms industry. Yet how could an enterprise withstand the pressure to meet such expectations without becoming entangled in building up arms capacity of little use and dubious value for a peacetime economy? It was an inextricable quandary for many arms companies at that time.

An outstanding example of this predicament was the manufacture of finished Widia tools. Although Krupp seemed to do everything to acquaint its customers with the applied technology, production even in the largest arms plants continued to lag far behind existing possibilities. The issue went beyond tool production, too. During the war it increasingly affected the significance of Widia in the manufacture of the penetrating cores of armor-piercing projectiles. By order of the Army High Command, Krupp therefore arrogated all Widia production to itself and expanded it within a year to a monthly output of 300,000 units, quintupling capacity. In return, the arms plants receiving these units had to cease all their own manufacture and cover their needs through Krupp. The Ministry for Armaments and Munitions facilitated the operation by agreeing to have it funded through additional price markups. Even more important, however, was the introduction of German industrial standards (DIN), thirty-six of which replaced four hundred sorts of Widia tool tips in use up to that time. These measures laid the foundation for serial manufacturing that more than doubled the output of each worker. The success proved Todt right, and he pressed for rationalization not only among the manufacturers but ever more insistently also among the clients in the Armed Forces High Command. His calls prompted rapidly intensifying attempts to reduce the diversity of types in the arms program and to standardize key intermediate products. This task became the focal point of the work in the main committees and rings (staffs of young arms managers fanatically loyal to the regime) that Albert Speer appointed at the lower command level of the Ministry of Armaments and Munitions after succeeding Todt as minister upon the latter's accidental death in early February 1942.

The new "business policy" was not confined to war production; it was intended also to set the course for the postwar period. Encompassing research, development, and diversified quality production as a context of innovation including consecutive serial manufacturing, the cast-steel factory could not be remodeled into an assembly-line plant. Instead, the adoption of the new manufacturing methods required the redesign of the group's structure even before the end of the war in order to give the firm a second line of business capable of simultaneously sustaining the new production line. Each new facility, however, had to be approved by the Reich Office of Economic Expansion, and the general ban on construction could be waived only for high-priority arms projects. Hence, the search was on for a strategy that combined peacetime planning and arms planning so that the one could help advance the other.

With the failure of the blitzkrieg against the Soviet Union and the entrance of the United States on the side of the Allies in World War II, Krupp had the opportunity to realize its plans in the eastern part of Germany. The prospect of a protracted war drove home how necessary it was to rationalize operations if Germany wanted to be a long-term match for those countries and their huge, highly developed capacity for the mass production of arms. During Todt's tenure as arms and munitions minister, the government was therefore still seeking industrial partners for its arms policy in order to build such capacity on the American model. At the Krupp factory in Essen, this challenge was taken up by the chief engineer, Erich Müller ("Cannon Müller"), who had been responsible for the entire manufacturing area since 1941. He had first-hand knowledge of the new processes for rationalizing the work process at Ford and had already put them into practice on a modest scale during his earlier work with the German State Railroad.

In October 1941 he launched the planning of an "assembly-line" factory for manufacturing 8.8 and 10.5 cm caliber guns—both types of which Krupp had developed itself. To sound out other firms about the scale, number, and kind of machine tools and about the requisite labor and most economical production methods, Krupp at once sought out the Gruson factory in Magdeburg, which had been engaged in serial manufacturing at a limited level since 1935. The planners quickly realized that the success of the "mass-production factory" would hinge primarily on two essentials corresponding to Henry Ford's basic principles: (a) the integration of the upstream operations, that is, the steel factory or block-casting plant, steel-casting plant, and sheet-rolling mill, and (b) the specification of the calibers, for each of which single-purpose machines were to be made. In November the engineering office of the Krupp factory in Essen decided on the size of the individual production lines and finishing shops and then waited for the designs of the specialized machines that had to be made in its own factory.

The great care that Krupp took in selecting the site for the Bertha factory in the midst of war attests more than anything else to the long-term nature of the planning, the perspective of which extended beyond the end of the conflict. The generously proportioned mass-production factory of Fordist conception would not only be able to buffer the state pressure on Krupp to manufacture arms, it would also open the option of mass-producing consumer goods. The entrepreneurial risk that this project indisputably meant for peacetime production and the costs of the hard lessons to be learned along the way could easily be passed on to the potential clients—the weapons offices of the three branches of the armed forces. The project seemed to offer yet another advantage: the new factory could be operated with unskilled workers, who, as foreign workers or forced labor, were more available on the "labor market" than were the high-quality workers otherwise crucial to Krupp.

The plan harbored risks as well, however. They lay not least in equipping production lines with single-purpose machines whose creation involved a tremendous amount of diversified quality machine manufacturing. True, their subsequent use in serial manufacturing offered high productivity at little operational expense, but by the fourth year of the war the long lead times entailed in making these specialized machines posed an obstacle. Even worse, the technical design of the production line and its effects on the mass manufacture of the machines proved to be nearly insurmountable difficulties. Few engineers in Germany had had experience in this area before the war, and Krupp's own modest credentials were limited to the Gruson plant. By the end of the war, this ability gap had been narrowed but never completely overcome. At the height of Germany's arms production, even in plants that had started out with assembly lines and state-of-the-art technology, the specialized machines never accounted for more than 9 percent of the equipment.[23] Repeated changes in planning and the high degree of flexibility that the machines had to have were senseless under these conditions. Right from the outset, they undermined the prospects for the success that could have been expected from automated production under ideal conditions. German arms planners, who constantly had to improvise and shift priorities in order to offset material and conceptual shortcomings, must have loathed being forever locked into almost unalterably large quantities of serial production, which called for both clear decision-making and the will to simplify and reduce the diversity of the weaponry. Neither precept could be counted on before 1944.

Even the labor question, which actually seemed to be solved at its root by the introduction of assembly-line manufacturing, became acute again. The majority of the serial-production plants were a world apart from an assembly-line approach that used single-purpose machines, so auxiliary workers performing simple manual manipulations and monotonous tasks were less sought than skilled workers, who could improvise to put the plant into operation and keep it running at least in the old workshop style. Instead of the desired, foolproof production of the Fordist type, Krupp was actually compelled to reinstall a small or intermediate mass-production system not in keeping with the laws of Fordist manufacturing. The first seven hundred people recruited by the Bertha factory in the German "protectorate" (formed by Hitler in 1939 from the Bohemian and Moravian parts of what had been Czechoslovakia) were therefore sent initially to Essen for training. Against this background, the local management responded less than enthusiastically when the Ministry of Armaments and Munitions in Berlin offered to staff the production operations with concentration camp inmates who were already assisting in the construction of the shop halls. (These prisoners were to be drawn from the Speer Engineering Staff of Organization Todt, the official network of agencies that Todt had built after 1937 for planning and administrating the Reich's major construction projects, regulating contracts with private companies, and mobilizing labor.) They were not needed under the prevailing conditions. The thought of maximizing efficiency through the extensive use of single-purpose machines, minute planning of all operations, and a work pace prescribed by the conveyor belt had to be abandoned little by little because thirteen major revisions had to be made by November 1943. The chaos continued unabated until October 1943, when Speer's so-called industrial self-administration—the network of committees and rings actually prevented any independent decisions—relieved

Krupp's management of its functions and took over the running of the Bertha factory. The action calmed the planning and enabled some of it to proceed on the authority of Speer's machinery of power.

The example of the Bertha factory shows that the efforts to introduce Fordist methods into German industry assumed colossal dimensions and went far beyond the classical fields of mass production such as the automotive industry. Many of the manufacturing methods experimented with during the war, however, could not be directly applied after 1945. They had been closely linked to arms production, such as aircraft-building, which underwent its Fordist conversion with Speer's fighter-plane program, and the construction of submarines, which Admiral Karl Dönitz had accelerated in 1943. The head of Speer's Main Committee for Shipbuilding, Otto Merker, a former manager of the truck manufacturer Klöckner-Humboldt-Deutz, revolutionized submarine construction by forcing the shipyards to make a radical switch to mass production modeled on American shipbuilding methods pioneered by Henry J. Kaiser.[24] Only three German shipyards experienced in submarine-building and known for the quality of their facilities were foreseen for the final assembly of decentrally prefabricated submarine cells. Although arms production was long forbidden after World War II and lost its earlier significance, it was during the war that German industry indisputably created for itself the option of using the Fordist production methods that it profitably exploited in the heyday of standardized mass production until the 1970s. As Krupp has clearly demonstrated in the postwar period, this achievement did not at all imply that German industry turned away from the principle of diversified quality production. In Essen, machine manufacturing and truck manufacturing had the choice of new methods that had been tediously worked out in Breslau, Magdeburg, and Bremen during the war.

Breakthrough to Mass Consumption

Although German industry was well prepared before 1945 to catch up with its American rival, the country was still a long way from actually doing so as far as Fordist methods of mass production were concerned. The conditions for such a breakthrough did not arise on the supply side until the Korean War and the subsequent boom on the world market. West Germany therefore arrived much later in the "age of mass consumption" (W.W. Rostow) than other industrialized countries did. The hallmark of this phase of economic development, which began in the United States in the Roaring Twenties, was the spread of durable consumer goods throughout the population. Aside from household appliances such as refrigerators and vacuum cleaners, the sector leading this cyclical boom in consumption was the car, whose increased sales in the United States had profound economic impacts, from road construction to a new settlement pattern.

In the 1950s, when West Germany entered the age of mass consumption, a new development was that durable consumer goods were no longer confined to middle and upper income groups; they infiltrated nearly all strata of the population as real income grew. In the second half of the 1950s, social position had ceased to play much, if any, role in determining ownership of some consumer goods, such as televisions, radio-phonographs, and refrigerators. Once again, the "democratization of consumption" won out, as it had since the nineteenth century for many durables formerly available only to privileged classes.

Between 1951 and 1961, the number of passenger cars in West Germany multiplied sevenfold from 700,000 to more than five million. The number of registered passenger cars exceeded that of motorcycles in 1954 and has remained ahead ever since, and the total number of cars surpassed that of motorcycles in 1957 for the first time. Consequently, the degree of motorization soared from 12.7 passenger cars per 1,000 inhabitants to 81.2, but it still lagged considerably behind that of other highly developed industrialized countries.[25] It was characteristic of this immense pent-up demand that the Federal Republic of Germany just reached the level of motorization in 1960 that the United States had already achieved in 1920.

In the 1950s private transport as a share of Germany's total passenger transport surged from 33.1 percent to 63 percent, whereas the share represented by the railroads shrank from 37.5 percent to 17.1 percent and that of local public passenger transport from 28.8 percent to 18 percent.[26] The share of employed persons among the new motorists rose from 8.8 percent in 1950 to 53 percent in 1960, and the share of the total number of passenger cars that they represented went from 12 percent to 54 percent. The private car became the password for social upward mobility, the middle-class feeling of freedom, opportunities for gainful employment, and social prestige. The ensuing changes for city planning, settlement policy, leisure time, communication behavior, economic structure, the environment, indeed for nearly all aspects of human life, revolutionized everyday reality.

If the internal dynamics of West Germany's economic miracle were home-made because the country removed inveterate developmental logjams and mobilized all its productivity reserves, then the unprecedented expansion of the world market in the 1950s and 1960s and West Germany's integration into it certainly promoted the process. The export volume of the sixteen OECD states grew only 1 percent from 1913 to 1950 compared to no less than 8.6 percent from 1950 to 1973. With the Federal Republic's exports expanding at rates ranging between -2.8 percent and +12.4 percent during that period,[27] the country both profited from and contributed to this prosperity. The foremost beneficiaries of this extraordinary trend were industries manufacturing high-quality machines, office and telecommunications systems, household appliances, and road vehicles. They reaped a twofold advantage: free access to their strategically important resources (e.g., raw materials, high-quality sheet steel, and single-purpose machines) and the ability to include the world market in their sales planning and thereby build and exploit the vast economies of scale that are the universal mark of Fordist production. Sure enough, trucks and aircraft became the key subcategory of West German export statistics. (The significance of aircraft was minimal in the 1950s.) The share of exports that these vehicles accounted for climbed from 4.8 percent in 1950 to 14.4 percent in 1965, both figures up from 2.6 percent in the mid-1930s.[28] Macroeconomic conditions after 1945 indisputably did much to encourage the introduction of Fordist methods of mass production.

Although the reconstruction of the consumer goods industry enjoyed absolute priority in the framework of a social market economy, it took until 1951 for consumption to recover the prewar level of 1936. The development potential of the West German domestic market therefore appeared promising. The attendant macroeconomic conditions, too, had changed completely. After 1951, West Germany's return to the world market was inexorable, and the automotive industry took a lively part in it. In the late 1950s West Germany's automotive industry posted more than half its turnover abroad, with the figure at the VW factory even exceeding 58 percent compared to the economy's average export rate of 16 percent. VW had a presence in no fewer than 160 countries and earned approximately half of West Germany's entire balance of payments.

"West German Fordism": The Volkswagen Case[29]

When the West German automotive industry resumed production after 1945, it knew the organizational and technological basics of Fordist assembly-line manufacturing well. The state of the art had been largely incorporated in the German factories of the Ford Motor Company and General Motors. The VW factory, too, had survived the war relatively unscathed. All the attacks and plundering shortly after the liberation of the forced laborers had destroyed only 10 percent of the machinery.[30] In August 1945 it was therefore possible to recommence operations with the production of twenty thousand passenger cars for use by the occupation powers. As early as 1949 the VW factory took the lead among the German automobile manufacturers. In that year it made forty thousand units, most of which were exported to Belgium, Switzerland, and Holland. The Ford plants in Cologne, which had still ranked first under the aegis of the military government in 1945 and 1946, fell to fifth place within three years, producing a mere one thousand cars a month (the Taunus model). Opel, far and away the leading German truck manufacturer before the war, was likewise overtaken by VW.[31]

Two main factors propelled the ascendance of the VW factory. First, it could systematically profit from the investments that had been made in it during the Third Reich. Although British experts were particularly skeptical of the

Beetle's quality and design, they were persuaded that both the production facilities and the equipment of the plant were sound and could operate successfully for years to come. American experts who inspected the company through the U.S. reparations program—the Field Intelligence Agency Technical (FIAT)—were also convinced that VW had the most modern equipment in the world and that the plant would have succeeded on the world market long before had the war not intervened.[32]

Second, until 1961 VW operated like a private company, without having private or public owners to claim part of its profits. It was therefore able to finance the factory's modernization from its own earnings. Problems arose only from the undersupply of specialized machines, particularly those that cost dollars to import. As late as the Korean crisis in 1951, bottlenecks with strategic resources such as stainless steel sheet of a particular width were still interrupting production and even leading to the closure of whole factories. The demand side, too, languished until the boom triggered by the Korean War in the early 1950s created the conditions necessary for mass sales, which had failed to materialize during the interwar periods (1919–1939 and 1945–1951) primarily because of high maintenance costs and inferior infrastructure. The tenacity required by the process of adapting to optimal Fordist organization is illustrated well by a typical indicator, the cycle time of car production. At 2.8 minutes in 1950, it was far off the classical one-minute pace that Ford's production methods in the United States had already achieved in the 1920s. VW did not catch up until 1953–1954.[33]

With the technological side of Fordist production methods having been mastered during World War II, they took root economically as well after 1945, giving the West German automotive industry the platform for a qualitative leap that unequivocally demonstrated the superiority of this approach. From 1950 to 1962, that is, during the reconstruction of the West German economy, prices for passenger cars even declined in absolute terms, whereas the general index of consumer prices went up by about 27 percent during the same period.[34] These facts are all the more amazing when it is remembered that the expense of the inputs most important to the production process of the automotive sector grew considerably in the 1950s. The price of steel shot up by around 100 percent. Wages rose even more—around 150 percent.[35] The decisive factor in the automotive industry's special development was its productivity, which increased an average of 9.37 percent annually in automotive manufacturing from 1953 to 1962. From 1952 to 1970, the corresponding value for that part of the industry was 9.4 percent compared to an annual increase of "only" 5 percent for economic productivity as a whole.[36] The automotive industry's share of the gross domestic product swelled from 1.7 percent in 1952 to 5 percent in 1960 and reached 8.9 percent in 1968. The number of passenger cars, vans, and station wagons produced in the Federal Republic of Germany climbed from approximately 220,000 in 1950 to 2.1 million in 1962, making

West Germany the world's second largest producer of motor vehicles as of 1956—ahead of Great Britain. Automobile production took place more and more within an oligopoly, with five companies controlling about 79 percent of the market. VW alone accounted for 30 percent of it.

From 1950 to 1954, when the Fordist methods of production were revived in the German automotive industry, VW expanded its production from 82,399 units to 202,174; Opel, from 59,990 to 148,242. Ford built 24,443 passenger cars in 1950, and in its hard battle for third place with Daimler-Benz (which made 48,816 cars in 1954) the company raised its production rate to 42,631. VW had always outstripped its American rivals in Germany. Whereas the Ford factories did not improve upon their prewar results until 1952, VW did everything it could from the start to keep pace with the automotive industry in the United States. The factory also took on the challenge of "Detroit automation," the clearest manifestation of which was the Cleveland Engine Plant that Ford opened in 1951. Detroit automation, however, sparked a furor and drew criticism in 1954 because its rigor prevented more flexible production methods. As a latecomer, VW was able to avoid these pitfalls, immediately profiting in 1954 and 1955 as it forged the typical German version of Fordism - American methods adapted to German conditions. The company's approach had three key characteristics:

1. VW returned to the origins of Fordism by confining its production to a single basic model until the early 1960s.
2. The VW factory developed a model of special industrial relations by cooperating closely with the Metalworkers Union (*Industriegewerkschaft Metall*) within the company. This strategy contradicted both the German principle that the outcome of collective bargaining apply to all the companies in the industry and the aloofness that Fordist companies in the United States adopted in their relations with the unions. But the homemade model of industrial relations made it possible to adapt the specific conditions of mass production to West Germany's rules of diversified quality production without having to forsake the advantages of Fordist wage policy.
3. VW put special value on the extension and quality of its service network at home and abroad. The factory thereby moved toward the prevailing pattern of operation, diversified quality production, and adopted one of its hallmarks.

The Fordist reorganization of the VW factory was preceded by close observation of the North American market and the corporate structures there. The results of this scrutiny were carefully evaluated in the summer of 1954. All the companies except Chrysler proved to have higher work performance than

VW did. Automation modeled on the American pattern of production would save VW around ten hours per passenger car.[37] The company strove for a system of continuous production lines that would couple all steps of the work process with each other, and the all-purpose machines hitherto in use were replaced with specialized machines wherever high numbers of pieces could be planned without frequent design alterations.[38] The automation of the factory focused solely on the production of Type I, the classical VW Beetle, which accounted for more than 75 percent of the group's entire production until 1961. Type II, the van, was closely related to the Beetle in design, however. Nothing resembling product diversification appeared at VW until the early 1960s. The parallel with the key function of the legendary Model T at Ford is striking. Of course, VW attached great value to the technological advance at its "flagship," more so than Henry Ford had done with his "Tin Lizzie."

Reorganization was tackled in 1954 and practically completed by the end of 1956. At the same time the company's management structure was overhauled on the basis of the American model. Lower management henceforth had greater authority to make *short-term* decisions for implementing general guidelines and the technical development of processes and the company's product. Quality control and development of basic corporate strategy remained in the hands of the top management, with subordinate levels of management being responsible for the organizational and technical realization of projected corporate objectives. One aim was to maximize autonomy at each level. The main department, "Technical Development," was structured and equipped in a manner that enabled it to work like an independent company, the idea being to add to the company's organizational flexibility and to differentiate this aspect of VW clearly from the mainstream of New Industries.

Wolfsburg, the seat of the VW factory, had no ambition to copy the highly integrated production complex of the American model—the Ford factories in River Rouge—which brought all stages of production under one roof, from the raw materials to the end product.[39] Instead, VW preferred the German practice of relying on a number of suppliers over whom the factory wielded substantial power. Because many of the suppliers sent more than 50 percent of their annual output to the VW factory, VW could directly influence their pricing. The relationship between the Wolfsburg factory and its suppliers was thus not exactly in keeping with the mutual trust and cooperation underlying the regional clusters in the field of diversified quality work. VW exploited their availability in order to create its own procurement base.

American and German traditions blended in the structure of industrial relations as well. VW's policy on collective bargaining was based essentially on the Fordist wage compromise, that is, on the coupling of wage hikes and growth in productivity. Introduced through the agreement between General Motors and the United Auto Workers Union in 1948, this linkage had meanwhile become something of a model.[40] As at Ford, privileges and positions within the VW plant hierarchy were allocated according to seniority. Remuneration criteria were based on job descriptions, not on personal qualifications. At VW, however, the issue was not about taking management's complete control over the work flow and extending it to the workplace as well. The factory had to take account of the historical fact in Germany that a company was seen primarily as a community in which cooperation between labor and capital also meant that management and the workforce shared power over the control of the workplace.[41] This power-sharing as an institution of labor relations reflects key elements of the classical German model: quality work and its accent on technical precision.[42] The fact that VW tried to live up to this tradition is apparent in both the management's distinct emphasis on community in the rhetoric of that time and the workforce's correspondingly strong feeling for corporate identity. The close cooperation with the works council and union representatives within VW also ensured that the factory was a leader in corporate social policy throughout the 1950s. The extent of payments above and beyond those agreed upon in the collective-bargaining process is documented best in a comparison between these special payments and the company's net profit as shown in the balance sheet, which totaled DM 689 million from 1950 through 1962. During the same period the factory's voluntary benefits to the workforce came to DM 630 million, the lion's share of which consisted in annual profit-sharing. In the 1950s the voluntary payments that the VW factory paid to its employees nearly equaled its net profit. This broad foundation of corporate social policy made it possible to tap reserves of workforce productivity that could not have been mobilized without these efforts.

From the outset, VW and the other major German automotive manufacturers looked to the world market. In this respect they differed from the great American model, which in the 1920s could rely largely on the domestic U.S. market. Its counterpart, the European Economic Community (EEC), could not initially fulfill this function for VW in the company's early years. France and Italy persisted in their national economic tradition by adopting protectionist measures that closed their domestic markets to their German competitor. When the Treaties of Rome were signed in 1957, only 16.4 percent of West Germany's passenger car exports were going to countries in what later became the EEC. Fully 35 percent of West Germany's car exports headed for the other European industrialized countries, including important buyers such as Sweden, Switzerland, and Austria of the rival European Free Trade Association (EFTA). In 1962 EFTA still accounted for a greater percentage of the value of West Germany's car exports (27.2) than the EEC did (25.6). In 1963 Heinrich Nordhoff, who chaired VW's managing board for many years, therefore considered the EEC, not EFTA, to be "a misfortune for Europe."[43] True, the "Dillon Round" of the General Agreement on Tariffs and Trade (GATT) effected a lasting reduction of the EEC's Common External Tariff for the automobile sector, the United States reduced its automobile duties from 8.5 to 6.5 percent, and the EEC lowered its rates from 29 to 22 percent. For West Germany, however, where customs had been only 13 to 16 percent, the new Common External Tariff of the EEC meant that the duties had to be raised.[44]

VW's export strategy thus acquired a special role. It drew on a network consisting of primary importers and dealers who independently organized the distribution of the Wolfsburg factory's vehicles to the appropriate national markets according to centrally planned and relatively narrow rules. On a few important markets it was necessary to organize sales through VW's own subsidiaries, and in some instances the cars had to be assembled abroad by VW itself. In the cases of Volkswagen Canada Ltd. (1952), Volkswagen of America, Inc. (1955), and Volkswagen France S.A. (1960), the sheer significance of the market was reason enough to take this approach. With Volkswagen do Brasil (1953), South African Motor Assemblers and Distributors, Ltd. (SAMAD) (1956), and Volkswagen (Australasia) Pty. Ltd. (1957), the creation of subsidiaries resulted from the economic policies of the respective countries, which encouraged import-substituting industrialization and thus made it difficult for importers to gain access to the market.[45] The VW factory was loath to yield to such pressure and often refused to build its own assembly plants.

By contrast, the American market has always been an integral part of VW's growth strategy, not just an extension of Germany's domestic market. When automation started, 8.2 percent of the company's total exports went to the United States, but by 1962 the U.S. market accounted for 31.2 percent and absorbed 22.2 percent of VW's domestic German automobile production. In the early 1960s nearly every fourth Beetle was exported to the United States.

This success indisputably stemmed from the increases in productivity that automation permitted after 1955. Combined with the strong West German currency, it made competitive pricing possible without resort to dumping. The decisive factor, though, was that the Beetle had found a niche that American corporations had left in the U.S. market until the introduction of the compact car in 1959. Beyond that year, the niche still left room for second cars.[46] Before the American car producers became completely convinced that likely sales and commensurate profit would justify investment in such vehicles, they were not prepared to finance the great expense of developing prototypes and designs, converting production, and procuring the special tools and machines necessary to install a new production line. Even after the relatively small U.S. car manufacturers, Studebaker and American Motors, came out with the first compact models (the Lark and the Rambler) in 1957 and after the three major U.S. corporations—General Motors, Ford, and Chrysler—followed with their own compact cars, VW was able to boost its percentage of the market from 1.7 in 1958 to 2.8 percent in 1962. Other importers, such as Renault, suffered severe losses.

Although improvement in productivity contributed much to VW's high degree of competitiveness, so did the quality of the service network that the company had meanwhile developed. The number of VW dealerships in the United States nearly doubled from 347 in 1957 to 687 in 1962. The price VW had to pay for such customer support was its chronic inability to supply all its export markets to the desired degree. Many delivery orders from the dealers went deliberately unmet so as to avoid overselling the Beetle in the United States and to keep pace with the burgeoning service organization, which was still sorely inadequate.

VW was equally resolute in resisting the temptation to produce the Beetle locally. Plans to use the assembly plant acquired from Studebaker in New Brunswick, New Jersey, for precisely that purpose were abandoned once and for all in January 1956 for lack of profitability, a decision by Heinrich Nord-hoff that conformed completely to the Fordist concept of large-scale series production. Production or assembly in the United States would have slowed the cost degression in Wolfsburg by siphoning more and more production away from German manufacturers, yet still would have failed to reach the batch sizes sufficient for Fordist mass production. Instead, VW set store in building up its service network, which Volkswagen of America was running purely as a business partnership from its headquarters in Englewood Cliffs, New Jersey.

The End of Mass Production

Starting with the automotive industry, Fordism continued its victorious march through West German industry. Alongside the nonmilitary use of nuclear energy ("Atoms for Peace"), automation was one of the topics that captured the imaginations of contemporaries. A sober assessment of automation's possible promise, risk, and danger did not come easily to most people, though individual observers well recognized the limited innovative power and range of automation and warned against exaggerating its significance.[47] The economic miracle did not result from the introduction of Fordist methods of mass production, but in this period of the resurgence they were the most conspicuous external manifestations of production. Important economic industrial sectors such as chemicals or electrical engineering likewise opened up to the Fordist production pattern without forsaking their commitment to quality production. The leading sector of West German industry, the automotive industry, heavily influenced the rules of the game in West German industrial society in order to ensure itself the wherewithal for its survival and to continue developing. This objective was most evident in the expansion of the transport infrastructure—ranging from Germany's motor expressways (the autobahns) to city-planning concepts centered on the private automobile as a transportation system.

In wage policy, too, the citadels of Fordist mass production led the way for the economy at large. Until the late 1960s, the trend in real wages practically paralleled the development of overall economic productivity. Thereafter, the two curves never diverged much either, except for the early 1970s. In Germany, Fordism also shaped the practice of codetermination by compelling the unions to be more flexible than in the past when dealing with companies and sectors not engaged in diversified quality work, the prevailing production regime. The new production method also created the need for a national and international anticyclical policy that could help regularize sales. All these behaviors and political objectives long outlived Fordism's crisis in the mid-1970s, though their pursuit was not always successful. Fordism itself thus produced the instruments that made it possible to cope with its demise in the West German economy.

The dynamics of the Fordist production pattern peaked in the 1960s and began to weaken worldwide a decade later. The causes of this decline are manifold and their relative importance difficult to judge.[48] Exogenous factors, such as the collapse of the Bretton Woods monetary and financial system, certainly had a role (though it would be going too far to consider Bretton Woods a part of the Fordist system). Undeniably, the oil-price shocks of the 1970s, the worldwide upward drift in grain prices, and other erratic fluctuations on the world markets were further external contributing factors, all of which undermined the long-term stability and growth of demand. The problems were compounded by changes in the structure of demand. These shifts reflected the fact that the needs structure was diversifying as incomes rose and made the sale of standardized, mass-produced goods difficult. In all likelihood, however, the situation stemmed also from a certain satiation of the very market sectors that had facilitated the spread of the Fordist production pattern in the first place many decades earlier. "Basic" durable consumer goods had spread to nearly all households in the United States, Japan, and many European countries, shifting demand to areas of the economy whose range of goods and services, as in the tertiary sector, lay largely outside the scope of standardized mass production. A particularly cogent example of this category was the manufacture of equipment in consumer electronics and computer processing, which became the leading product markets in the 1970s.

Diversification and globalization—the ways in which the affected manufacturers responded to the crisis—could not really eliminate the obstacles for long. By splitting up product profiles and increasing the number of sites, they actually reduced the odds of achieving the economies of scale that had once constituted the comparative advantage of this production pattern. At first glance, it therefore seemed that mass production would be superseded by a return to craft methods, which had survived at the margins of Fordist production. However, one would grossly misread the character of twenty-first-century industrial production by reducing it to the manual production of luxury goods, prototypes, and small-lot series. Craft production is certainly able to exploit the advantages of technological innovation in order to survive and go on to open up new markets, particularly when it can build on the synergies of established industrial districts. Just as the electric motor promoted the decentralization of production and, hence, the survival of craftwork vis-à-vis big industry in the late nineteenth century, today's new, flexible technologies such as computer-aided linking of design, work-planning, and manufacturing (CAD systems) may offer flexible specialization that can open new perspectives in some of the crafts. On most markets in Germany, though, the economic alternative to standardized mass production is not craftwork but rather diversified quality work. Its significance in absolute terms has never waned, even during the heyday of Fordism. As the age of mass production ends, diversified quality production seems better adapted than ever to the competitive conditions on the world market. It is, as German automotive manufacturing shows, well on the way to regaining the ground it had lost to Fordism.

German manufacturers of luxury, fashionable, and custom-made, top-quality, high-performance automobiles still set the standard in their class throughout the world. Although DaimlerChrysler, BMW, Audi, Porsche, and similar companies may be much smaller than mass producers such as General Motors and Toyota, they control two thirds of the upscale segment of the world market and make the German automotive industry as a whole one of Germany's strongest export sectors. They owe their competitiveness primarily to two conditions. First, they are embedded in established regional clusters and a concomitant, highly specialized, dense network of suppliers, an arrangement that enables this industry to diversify its production and adapt it closely to the purchaser's individual wishes. In this high-performance segment of a sector that until only recently embraced the vision of standardized mass production and its growing economies of scale, the finished vehicles are now seldom completely identical. Second, the manufacturers of sports cars and luxury cars are particularly the ones who profit from the quality-enhancing basic conditions of the German production regime, from high-performance motor expressways to codetermination. The strength of Germany as a home to industry is borne out by the fact that the 1998 takeover of Chrysler, described in politically correct language as a "merger," was executed expressly under German law. The Stuttgart-headquartered corporation used the announcement in London as the occasion to sing the praises of codetermination, which has been experienced as "very beneficial" in the parent company.[49] It is not surprising that the most recent turnaround of the Chrysler side of the corporation in the United States is following the Stuttgart model. Like the Japanese automotive industry, German car manufacturing has managed to overcome severe backwardness and has found its own version of Fordism, one that fully capitalizes on its specific institutional conditions. In its domain of high-performance cars, it offers the model of "best practice" to follow on the world market.

3. Codetermination
The German Response to the Agency Problem

Judgment on the effects that codetermination has on the German economy vacillates between two oddly inconclusive, but by no means contrary, assessments. The first one emphasizes codetermination's irenic influence, which serves Germany's social system of production in the same manner that a functioning welfare state does. This view is supported by at least fifty years of positive experience with industrial democracy but avoids a clear statement about its economic value. The second assessment, often readable between the lines of well-meaning commentary, amounts to an assertion that codetermination in the waning industrial age is—like the welfare state—threatening to become obsolete because its core functions are intimately linked with the industrial economy and will therefore go down with it. This opinion rests on the basic assumption that the western world stands at the end of an era whose foundations were laid in the Industrial Revolution of the late eighteenth century and whose distinctly German traits have produced a system of industrial governance unique in the world. These two judgments, if they pertain at all, do not describe the economic function of codetermination but rather, at best, one of its most obvious effects.

Codetermination in Germany has two roots. One reaches deep into the peculiarities of the German path to industrialization. In the race to modernity, Germany is well known to have been one of the latecomers that had to develop their own institutions and organizations in the nineteenth century[50] in order to catch up with the pioneer, England—or better, leapfrog ahead of it. Given the positive associations that Germany had had with welfare-state traditions, the social question in the nineteenth century became especially urgent there. Certain kinds of institutional and organizational solutions were needed in order to protect emerging industrial society from the destructive effects of industrial dynamics. These "premiums for eliminating the risks of revolutionary twitches in the body politic"[51] included the German empire's occupational safety and health policy. This program ran right through the imperial message of 4 February 1890, in which Emperor William II promised to provide a legal framework for workers' committees to exercise codetermination rights of the kind that stemmed from workers' involvement in the administration of company health insurance offices. Although the relation between the workers and the state organs was thus predefined in the imperial message, the amended industrial code of 1 June 1891 did not mandate the introduction of workers' committees after all. The amendment of the Prussian Mining Act finally did so in 1905, at least in the mining sector. Whereas workers' committees there encountered bitter resistance by the mining companies, 10 percent of all private companies with more than twenty employees, including many large companies, had voluntarily established such groups by then. They assisted the directors of the health insurance offices, which in most enterprises were also accepted as the workers' representatives for mediating general grievances.[52] More than half of all machine manufacturing companies—one of the New Industries—had taken this step, and two thirds of them had rated the influence of the committees positively.[53] Recognition of the workers' economic organizations as authorized representatives of their members' interests was finally accorded by the Auxiliary Service Act of 5 December 1916, which granted rights of codetermination to the mandatory workers' committees in companies with more than fifty workers employed in areas important to the war effort.

The Weimar Republic then introduced rights of codetermination at all three levels of interest intermediation: on the shop floor, with the Works Councils Act of 1920; at the sectorial level, with ZAG; and at the national level, with the Provisional National Economic Council conceived of in Article 165 of the Weimar constitution. The contentious situation surrounding each of these achievements underscored their political character and social mission, at least more so than they highlighted the necessity of codetermination as a matter of corporate policy and business economics. In post-1945 occupied Germany, too, this preeminence of the sociopolitical dimension marked the British insistence on granting employees equal voice on the supervisory boards of the iron and steel industry. It also underlay the legislative institutionalization of rights to participate in decision-making in that sector (the *Montanmitbestimmungsgesetz* of 1951), which reflected a singular domestic and foreign-policy constellation arising from the Korean crisis.[54]

Although the importance of stable, cooperative labor relations became readily apparent to most entrepreneurs during the long 1950s, and although codetermination was one of the essentials for long-term productivity gains, growth, and competitiveness,[55] the orthodox liberal persuasion continued to dominate the economic theory of industrial relations. Indeed, it still does,[56] with codetermination seen as a strengthening of bargaining power and, hence, of the unions' monopoly on the market. If a union can behave like the holder of a monopoly, it will try to maximize the wages of its members, whereas all the affected company can do is choose the employment level at which it earns maximum profit. From this perspective, the consequences are price rises and misallocations of resources. As long as codetermination seemed suitable for preserving the precarious balance of the social question in industrial society, dyed-in-the-wool liberals were quite able to accept it for the sake of social peace and the stability that codetermination was evidently able to bring to labor relations. From this angle, too, however, it follows that the end of industrial society and the declining importance of material production mean that codetermination loses sociopolitical legitimacy. It was created as a means of industrial stabilization, and as such, its effect seems to reach as far as the epochal significance of the Industrial Revolution itself, which has long since ceded its rank to the new paradigm of the Second Economic Revolution.

Against this backdrop, codetermination's economic value really boils down to the degree of importance that long-term cooperative labor relations have in the economic process of value creation, or more precisely, the level of transaction costs. Such relations are evident in the way that employees and their interests are organizationally tied into the company. To ensure that they are, and to forge cooperative labor relations, employers may be prepared to pay the employees higher wages than is customary or to give broad guarantees of job security. Employers thereby enable themselves to invest in the basic and continued training of their employees. This investment is a prerequisite for increasing profits, especially under the conditions created by the rapid structural shift to the "knowledge society." Reduced fluctuation and intensified motivation among employees compensate for cost inflation.[57]

Asymmetrical distribution of knowledge on the shop floor is another attribute of production relations in the knowledge society. Nonmaterial production and the scientifically grounded qualifications it requires usually depend on expert knowledge, which is difficult to replace and whose productive use in the work process is not easy to control. Optimal performance by an employee with expert knowledge cannot be formulated in precise contractual terms, nor could such contracts be cost-effectively monitored and enforced. In short, the situation is a classical variation of the agency problem. Management is thus steadily losing its ability to exercise absolute control over the workplace at somewhat reasonable cost. And when conflict arises, employees possessing specialized knowledge can damage the company more than could the classical industrial worker, who had only generalized—and thus easily replaceable—knowledge. If the Leninist maxim of "Trust is good, control is better" applied to the industrial context, the opposite is true under these new conditions. Moreover, control is the more expensive option. As a result, management and employees or their respective representatives share control over the workplace. Profit-sharing and codetermination provide for the necessary agreement on the utility function of "principal" and "agent."

Long-term, stable, and low-conflict labor relations are important for yet other reasons, particularly in times of rapid structural change. A high level of qualification and initiative among the employees gives the enterprise great incentive to make cost-intensive investment in fixed assets. They also ensure that these investments can be fully used and amortized. High fixed costs can thereby be turned into low unit costs. Investments in new technology raise the productivity of the company, expanding its share of the market and boosting profits. Adequate employee participation in these profits strengthens cooperative labor relations.

The new interpretative approach in research on industrialization and the resulting redefinition of the periods into which the race into the postindustrial economy is divided can improve on past answers to some of the open questions in the history of German codetermination. To begin with, German unions made their breakthrough as mass organizations in the 1890s, the decade of the unions. At that time there also emerged institutional patterns, behaviors, mentalities, organizational principles, and structures that are said to still exist today. The unions, too, underwent the extensive, revolutionary process of institutional change that set up radically new rules of economic activity within two decades. After the turning point in 1879, for example, the principle of cooperation replaced that of competition in interest intermediation and macroeconomic organizational policy, state mobilization replaced *laissez faire* in economic policy, corporative self-governance supplanted organized self-help in social policy, corporatism at least partially displaced parliamentarianism as the vehicle for interest mediation, and "enlightened" protectionism superseded Manchester-style liberal free trade.[58] Much of what these changes created in terms of new, basic institutional conditions was later claimed by the labor movement—occasionally despite the historical facts—to be part of its own political worldview and the result of its own political work, and not only in the exceptional circumstances of August 1914. The desire for codetermination fit seamlessly into this new macroeconomic organizational policy of the coordinated market economy, although none of the three levels of interest intermediation was ever possible until the Weimar Republic. This desire reflected the wish to achieve recognition of the heightened importance of the human factor in the production process of the ascendant New Industries, in which science and technology created a new, revolutionary foundation for gains in productivity—for Douglass C. North's Second Economic Revolution. Therein lies the second root of German codetermination.

On the shop floor, codetermination became a useful arrangement for both diversified quality work and standardized mass production. Although it was tailored more to the former, it had its merits for the latter as well. Under Taylorism and Fordism skilled workers were not threatened by deskilling as much as by the loss of their relatively autonomous position at the workplace. Codetermination compensated for a lack of motivation, particularly since the $5 minimum wage that Ford introduced in Detroit in 1915 seemed unrealistic in Germany for the foreseeable future. But codetermination and its equivalents were even more important outside the still rudimentary sector of mass production. Under the alleged pressure of German rationalization, which was said to require investment mainly in human capital because of limited sales markets and inadequate capital assets, the employers in New and Old Industry alike counted on shop-floor cooperation. The concepts for obtaining it ranged widely. Heavy industry, for example, sought to integrate "high-quality workers" into the "factory community," for which purpose it created the German Institute for Technical Training (Deutsches Institut für Technische Arbeitsschulung, DINTA) in 1925. Some parts of the unions supported the plant social policy linked with the technocratic concept known as "human economy" (*Menschenökonomie*). There were also specific forms of codetermination practiced by the works councils in many plants of New Industries.[59]

Hence, a basic current of cooperation remained beneath the contentious political surface of the Weimar Republic even after the early failure of ZAG, the organization that had been intended to fill the political power vacuum during the years of revolution. The spectrum of this interaction extended from practical collaboration on the shop floor to ultimately futile attempts to somehow revive ZAG. The more quickly pessimism welled up in industry in the 1930s and the more rapidly the end of the industrial economy seemed to near, the greater was the belief in a new era of economic development in which the human factor had a key role to play. Cooperation at the workplace—including the "plant family scheme" (*Betriebsgemeinschaft*), the form into which it was perverted by the Nazis—seemed to fit the bill. With the uncertainty about how production and competition would develop, and with the ever more complex technological changes taking place at the time, every investment decision had to be based more on planned entrepreneurial and corporative coordination in the innovation process than on market coordination. The swifter the advance of nonmaterial production and the division of labor in the twentieth century, the steeper the rise in transaction costs and, hence, the greater the need for institutional regulations and conventions for controlling such costs.[60]

To be sure, the spark of the new production methods seldom leapt from New Industries to the rest of Germany's crisis-ridden economy, marked as it was by the conditions spawned by the two world wars and economic chaos. After dynamic beginnings under the empire, nonmaterial production and the conditions for innovative productivity did not spread to the tertiary sector and the economy as a whole. In fact, during the interwar period they even declined relative to what was happening elsewhere at the same time, notably in the United States. The pioneer of the Second Economic Revolution nevertheless held to its course into the postindustrial age. Once established, the institutional context did not change more than incrementally, despite all exogenous shocks. Nor did codetermination—or better, the principle of cooperative labor relations within companies. Much the same was also true for other forms of cooperative labor beyond the shop floor (e.g., ZAG), though in a somewhat milder way. Codetermination in Germany, quite apart from its organizational manifestation in the Weimar Republic and its perversion under the Third Reich, belongs to the New Economy's institutional arsenal, which has repeatedly created new organizational frameworks. Admittedly, the legal and organizational form that emerged for the principle of codetermination after 1945 was shaped by the political conditions of the times, but it was consistent with the economic needs of that period.

At the dawn of the twenty-first century, it is almost a truism that the value of human capital is measured not only in terms of its own quantity and quality but primarily in terms of a society's aptitude for sociability.[61] Without it, cooperation is feasible only by means of formal rules, regulations, and coercion. The resulting costs (transaction costs) escalate with the complexity of the tasks a national economy must perform to be successful on the market (including the world market). In practice, mistrust thus has the same effect as a tax on economic activity. From the outset, the purpose of introducing codetermination in Germany was to minimize these costs. With the advent of New Industry in the twentieth century, the capacity for cooperation only gained importance. This sociability helps explain why the basic features of the German production regime, including codetermination, have survived all the political catastrophes of its era.[62] Codetermination is constitutive not only for the German system of industrial relations but also for the dual training system and wage policy (the practice of having the results of collective bargaining apply to all companies in an industry). They facilitate technology transfer within industries, standardization, and other features of the intercompany system in Germany. Codetermination thereby becomes an essential part of the coordinated market economy.

The high value attached to the economic culture of trust helps explain why new organizational forms of codetermination—whether in the iron, coal, and steel industry or in the Labor-Management Relations Act of 1952—were swiftly accepted despite their controversial beginning. Above all, it explains their consolidation and practical development beyond their original legal setting. Such interlinkages also smoothed the way for the introduction of employee rights to an equal voice on the supervisory boards of the iron and steel industry. This codetermination owes less to British insistence after World War II than to German tradition. The chief actor behind the new concept was the director of the German trusteeship of the iron and steel industry, Heinrich Dinkelbach. Not only was he a former managing board member of Vereingte Stahlwerke and thus an expert on conditions in the steel industry, he was also a devout apostle of Catholic social doctrine and thus a representative of corporatist codetermination, although the steel industry used to prefer other organizational solutions.

The new perspective taken in historical research sharpens the eye for other impacts as well. The origins of cooperative institutional arrangements—more narrowly, codetermination—do not lie in the rationale of the bygone industrial age. They are foundations of New Economies, whose patterns of nonmaterial productivity are becoming ever more apparent as old industry's share of employment and value creation through material production dramatically declines.[63] The economic significance of codetermination and other forms of institutional cooperation does not stem solely from their calming, mediating, and sociopolitical function but also from what they do to contain and reduce production costs and transaction costs within complex market and production processes. Of course, this realization does not compel anyone to cling to the outmoded organizational forms of codetermination. Appropriate institutional arrangements can surely be cast in other organizational molds as well. According to the laws of "asset specificity," however, turning to such alternatives entails considerable cost.[64] Because institutional change cannot be planned, success would by no means be guaranteed. There are thus many reasons for the German model of codetermination to continue developing along "path-dependent" lines—if the capacity for cooperation that has accrued over the preceding fifty years or more is not to be written off completely. As long as this path corresponds to the overall development of the social system of production, it will not lead to anachronisms of industrial society. It will instead ensure purposeful expansion of the institutional groundwork of New Industry that was laid in the late nineteenth century.[65]

4. Social Market Economy
Production-Related Design of the Organization and Rules of the Economy

One of the most sharply drawn front-line positions in the culture clash between social systems of production is the role that government has, for it differs from one economy to the next. From the stance of economic history, it is difficult to justify the antithesis of market and state, of deregulation and regulation , as a struggle between two polar patterns of economic order competing to find the most efficient method of steering the economy. In reality, there is just as little functional antagonism between the market and the state as there is between the market and business. As shown in 1937 by Ronald H. Coase, who won the Nobel Prize for economics in 1991, companies legitimate their existence by helping reduce production costs, especially transaction costs, and hence by satisfying economic needs at lower costs than would be possible without them "on the market." He pointed out that companies do these things by guaranteeing contracts, internalizing property rights, and building trust.

State economic policy operates no differently. The government conceives and implements rules and standards to which the majority of economic actors voluntarily submit in order to make their action more calculable, certain, and cost-effective than the markets can without the state's involvement. The essential core of every economic policy is therefore in the design of the institutional context, no matter how necessary interventions in the economic process (i.e., regulatory policy) may be from case to case. German political economists, who argued on the basis of institutional economics, asserted that the state's capacity and function as "the most important intangible capital" had, by the turn of the twentieth century, already become a factor "whose direct or indirect indispensability to all significant economic production was clear enough."[66] Combined with Adolph Wagner's postulate that the "preventive principle" in economic policy should supersede the "repressive principle," according to which the state's task is merely to correct economic disorders,[67] this insight did not come out of the blue at the end of the nineteenth century. A new organizational context was required by the symbiosis that had been achieved between science and business in the production process (the knowledge society) and by the stability needed for progressive, worldwide market integration and dynamics (globalization), interrupted though they were several times during the century. Establishing a production pattern such as diversified quality production, which can be seen as the response to these challenges, was all but unimaginable without the massive collective input that government offers. The scale of what was clearly necessary but that lay outside accessible market structures ranged from the material infrastructure and secure legal footing of voluntarily developed institutions to basic research and the regulation of occupational qualification. Within the social system of production, the government thereby still fell far short of achieving primacy over the economy, but it became increasingly responsible for tasks that were reconcilable with neither the theory nor the practice of liberal economic policy.

The heart of German economic policy in the twentieth century was the state's production-related frameworking of the social and economic system. Ever since the 1870s, its preferred fields have included foreign trade; infrastructural policy in the broadest sense; regional development policy, which had both an economic and social dimension; and an occupationally centered education and training policy intended to develop new capacities of human capital. The purpose of this government macroeconomic organizational policy was to nurture the economy mostly by providing general input and setting rules intended to encourage private economic activity, influence its siting, and design it to be more productive than in the past. A distinction of this postliberal economic policy was that it recognized the significance of nonmaterial production as a source of powerful, hitherto unknown currents of productivity and thereby accommodated the rise of the New Economy, which appeared early in Germany. An additional novelty was the insight that appropriate institutions and standards (i.e., ones that reduced transaction costs) as collective input do not create value directly but do create productive forces crucial to overall economic productivity in the long term.

Significantly, neither the government nor the market controlled some of the economic innovations of the late nineteenth century. From the late nineteenth century on, it was actually the cities, local communities, and districts that controlled the lines of business that operated on the most dynamic markets—the electricity companies and other utilities, for example, and regional lending (the savings banks). The local authorities selectively used these parts of the economy to shape local welfare and development policy, an approach known as municipal socialism. State economic policy-makers could not remain indifferent to the opportunities to succeed in this highly innovative and rapidly growing sector of economic development. They saw the broad field of local services and material infrastructure as the ideal place to mobilize new resources and productivity reserves by investing in factors that could advance economic modernization deep within Germany's economic space—right in line with Friedrich List's theory of productive forces. Every pfennig that helped permit this economic activity in the poorer communities, too, was expected to have a developmental snowball effect far exceeding most alternative uses of public expenditures. This effect required a functioning system of interregional revenue equalization of the kind that characterized German business throughout the century. This practice, a solid part of German economic structures that still weathers criticism, demonstrates that equality of living conditions and balanced deployment of productive forces are traditionally key objectives of German economic policy. Hence, only a small part of public investment lies within the responsibility of the central government.

This arrangement has been particularly true of funding for science and research. With the emergence of science-based industries as leading sectors of the economy and nonmaterial production—the paradigm of twentieth-century economic development—such support became the focus of production-related design of the social and economic framework. The link between collective knowledge production and economic productivity was not always explicit, but the more "labor," specifically "science," gained importance as a production factor, the more it became necessary for government economic policies to take account of that connection by creating the institutional context for their use and by providing resources to foster the "production" of new qualifications and stocks of knowledge. Nowhere was the tie between science, technology, and business as close as in imperial Germany. The country systematically supported not only big industry but also "large-scale science," which Theodor Mommsen saw in 1890 as a "necessary element of our cultural development" and which Adolf von Harnack elaborated into the large scientific enterprise named the Kaiser Wilhelm Society.[68]

In principle, war, revolution, and the transition from the German empire to the Weimar Republic altered little in the concept of German macroeconomic organizational policy. The institutional setting for its execution did not change appreciably, either. More important, the production regime that had developed under the empire remained almost completely intact. The corporatist status of organized labor had evidently taken hold during the war and had become entrenched once and for all in the German Revolution of November 1918.

As important as government economic policy may have been in promoting economic success by influencing basic conditions and, increasingly, by intervening directly, it left the primacy of business untouched. In the end, self-administration and autonomy with respect to organizational matters and interest intermediation stood in sharp contrast with the efficiency of the coordinated market economy under the Weimar Republic. This contrast had essentially objective reasons that caused the coordinated market economy to capitulate to a number of domestic and nondomestic problems that finally blocked its dynamics and intensified distributional conflicts. However, these problems also stemmed from the bureaucratization and "complacency" (Hegel's word: *Verhausung*) of their corporatist structure, for which critical contemporaries eventually had only sarcastic words.[69] But the decisive reason that the government ultimately assumed final responsibility for the outcome of economic processes was the failure of corporatist interest inter-mediation to cope with the catastrophe of the Great Depression. In Germany, it was no coincidence that this transition to a new role for government coin-cided with the National Socialist seizure of power and the rise of the Nazi regime. The new government did not have to overcome resistance to accom-plish the shift. With the deplorable collapse of private business's influence on the labor market, the major politicoeconomic schools of thought widely rec-ognized the alleged necessity of accepting the primacy of the state in 1933. The state therefore represented the common denominator to which the terrible experience of the Great Depression had reduced all concepts of eco-nomic policy in Germany.

This outcome is not surprising for the dominant current of German statist economic policy, in which regulatory thinking revolved around the political science tradition associated with the historical school of political economics represented by Adolph Wagner and Gustav Schmoller. Glorifying the road to modernism in Prussia and other German states, the social conservatives in the Social Policy Association wanted to believe the state capable of performing miracles, and there was no task they were unwilling to hand over to it in their goal of co-opting the labor movement. They were decried for their efforts, but the labor movement, too, regarded the state as "society's only effective and empowered organization" that could "in principle substitute the socialist prin-ciple of planned production for the capitalist principle of free competition."[70] The labor movement therefore considered its foremost task to be to act "with the help of the state, with the help of the intentional social arrangement, to take this economy organized and led by capitalists and transform it into an econ-omy led by the democratic state."[71] For both currents of German economic policy—the conservative statist and the socialist—it was therefore relatively easy to accommodate the primacy of the state.

The Great Depression cut deepest, however, into the prevailing doctrine, liberalism. It became necessary to shed familiar ideas about the liberal state and orient economic thinking critically to the reality of a state that intervenes in the economy, which Walter Eucken judged to be very "rarely capable" of "bringing pure state interest to bear."[72] The way to escape the "swamping of capitalism" decried by Eucken was not to reject interventionism per se but rather to develop a "liberal interventionism."[73] He and other reformers such as Alexander Rüstow understood the term to mean "taking action that is pre-cisely the opposite of that taken earlier, that is, not contrary to market laws but rather in the direction of market laws, not to maintain the old but rather to bring about the new state of affairs, not to delay but rather to accelerate the natural process."[74] Regulatory policy had traditionally triggered liberal anxieties about intervention. Although the state's role in designing the social and economic system's organization and rules was recognized, more by Adam Smith than by his epigones, it was explicitly relegated to a place subordinate to the actors on the market. The Great Depression put an end to such reservations. In Rüstow's culminating words at the Dresden meeting of the Association for Social Policy in 1932, "In any case, the new liberalism defensible today demands a strong state, a state above the economy, above the vested interests, where it belongs."[75]

The response in Germany to the challenge of the Great Depression was therefore not sought in the realm of economic theory, as in the Great Britain of John Maynard Keynes, but rather in the reorganization of the economic order. The liberal concept of reform dates back further than 1945; it has been one of the steadfast alternatives of German economic policy since the early 1930s. In addition to the call for stable and unrestricted currency exchange, it encompassed the entire legal system, focusing on competition, freedom of trade, freedom of movement, freedom of consumption, freedom of contract, and contract law. In principle, this scope had profound consequences for the social system of production in Germany. But they were neither discussed theoretically nor acted upon after 1945.

It seems that the Federal Republic of Germany became something of an exception within Europe when it embarked on a *Sonderweg* with its economic policy in 1949. By embracing the social market economy, West German economic policy-makers wanted not only to overcome traditional liberal notions of the economic order and reform the principle of competition inherent in the market economy. They also sought to offer alternatives to Keynesian countercyclical fiscal and budgetary policy and turned in particular against Keynesianism's German manifestations, which had arisen very early in the shadow of the Great Depression. More than anything, West German economic policy stressed the paramount importance of setting the overall context in which business is conducted. A strong state was expected to guarantee markets the basic institutional conditions that were commensurate with the prevailing social system of production. Reform liberalism, too, thus followed in the tradition of this macroeconomic production-related organizational policy as practiced in Germany since the days of the empire. The social market economy is the result of a long learning process that drew lessons from a number of crises and successes experienced by Germany's industrial economy. They included the realization that the macroeconomic production function could no longer be stabilized without the primacy of the state as a nonmaterial factor of production. If the social market economy has remained the German doctrine of economic policy despite the profound change the system has undergone in its first fifty years, this endurance owes partly to continuity in the production-related frameworking of the economy.

Although the German path to the New Economy is inconceivable without its integration in the collective flow of goods attributable to this approach, that does not mean unconditional acceptance of every protracted, rampant increase of state influence on the economy. Having originated in specific nineteenth-century conditions that do not pertain now, many economic activities of the state, local communities, and regional authorities no longer automatically seem to warrant continuation. The areas involved include public electric utilities, the transport and communications sector, financial institutions, the health-care system, public and private safety, and the broad field of education, training, and research. The more that structural change has moved macroeconomic demand for goods and services into these traditionally state-run sectors in Germany, the less the state has been able to respond appropriately on the supply side.

A number of restrictions prevent the public sector from flexibly adapting its economic activity to market conditions and from expanding its capacity to meet increasing demand. Legal and mental vestiges of cameralist accounting, lack of management practice, underdeveloped awareness of costs, legal and political resistance to deregulated pricing of public goods and services, and, most of all, political constraints on using tax revenues to finance additional jobs make the public sector appear unsuitable for managing the very areas of the economy that are the most dynamic. Privatization usually seems a proven remedy—provided it does not impinge on the state's economic role where it is still important in the functioning and efficiency of the social system of production. Savings banks are such an exception, for their commitment to the common weal and to regional tasks still seems indispensable to the comprehensive financing of investment in a national economy as decentralized and oriented to small business as Germany's is. Above all, however, a production regime based on diversified quality work is inconceivable without a training system whose unrestricted access guarantees equal economic opportunity as well as the full mobilization and use of human capital.

Notes

1. Michael E. Porter, *The Competitive Advantage of Nations* (London: The Free Press, 1990); see also the corresponding special study on Germany: Claas van der Linde, *Deutsche Wettbewerbsvorteile* (Düsseldorf: Econ, 1992).
2. Soskice, "Globalisierung."
3. Albert, *Capitalisme.*
4. Fukuyama, *Trust.*

5. France represents a third, quite different pattern that can be described as a market system jointly coordinated by the government, companies, and elites. However, it is less secure and more in flux than the other two patterns. See Bob Hancké and David Soskice, "Coordination and restructuring of large French firms: The evolution of French industry in the 1980s" (WZB Discussion Paper FS I 96-303, 1996), Wissenschaftszentrum Berlin für Sozialforschung.

6. North, *Institutions*, pp. 6-7.

7. On the debate about the industrial state, see Barkin, *Controversy*.

8. In this context, Douglass C. North speaks of a Second Economic Revolution. See North, *Structure*.

9. Soskice, "Globalisierung," pp. 207–208.

10. On the current dimensions of this concept, see Wolfgang Streeck, "On the institutional conditions of diversified quality production," in Egon Matzner und Wolfgang Streeck (Eds.), *Beyond Keynesianism, The Socio-Economics of Full Employment* (Aldershot, Hants, England: Elgar, 1991), pp. 21–61.

11. Ibid., p. 31.

12. Frederick Winslow Taylor, *Principles of Scientific Management* (New York: Harper & Brothers, 1911).

13. Friedrich von Gottl-Ottlilienfeld, *Fordismus. Über Industrie und technische Vernunft* (Jena: Gustav Fischer, 1926), p. 12.

14. See Anita Kugler, "Von der Werkstatt zum Fließband. Etappen der frühen Automobilproduktion in Deutschland," in *Geschichte und Gesellschaft* 13 (1987), 304–339; see 334–335.

15. Petition to the German Reichstag concerning the amendment of customs legislation, 8 July 1925, Reichstag Proceedings, stenographic accounts, Attachments (Drucksachen).

16. Anita Kugler, *Arbeitsorganisation und Produktionstechnologie der Adam-Opel-Werke (von 1900 bis 1929)*, Preprint, International Institute for Comparative Social Research (IIVG)/Labor Policy, Wissenschaftszentrum Berlin, 1985, IIVG pre 85-202, pp. 53–57.

17. Fred Ledermann, *Fehlrationalisierung – Der Irrweg der deutschen Automobilindustrie seit der Stabilisierung der Mark* (Stuttgart: Pöschel, 1933), p. 27.

18. Another special characteristic of Fordist mass production in Germany stems from development in the Soviet zone of occupation (subsequently the German Democratic Republic, GDR). Authorities there vigorously pressed ahead with the standardization of industrial production in the automotive industry, though not primarily in that sector. The GDR, however, essentially had only its own, small domestic market. Moreover, the country restricted the concept of Fordism exclusively to technology and management.

19. Karl-Heinz Ludwig, *Technik und Ingenieure im Dritten Reich* (Düsseldorf: Athenäum/ Droste, 1979), p. 462. For an international comparison, see Mark Harrisson (Ed.), *The Economics of World War II: Six Great Powers in International Comparison* (Cambridge, England: Cambridge University Press, 1998).

20. Werner Abelshauser, "Rüstungsschmiede der Nation? Der Kruppkonzern im Dritten Reich und in der Nachkriegszeit 1933 bis 1951," in Lothar Gall (Ed.), *Krupp im 20. Jahrhundert: Die Geschichte des Unternehmens vom Ersten Weltkrieg bis zur Gründung der Stiftung* (Berlin: Siedler, 2002), Pt. 3, especially Ch. 5.

21. Ibid., p. 447.

22. Ibid., p. 270.

23. Monthly report of the Specialized Machine-Tool Committee for December 1943, 21 January 1944, BA Berlin, R 3/491.

24. In the United States, Kaiser successfully transferred Ford's assembly-line production methods from automotive manufacturing to shipbuilding, enabling his shipyards to construct ships in as little as $4\frac{1}{2}$ days. See Edward R. Zilbert, *Albert Speer and the Nazi Ministry of Arms: Economic Institutions and Industrial Production in the German War Economy* (London: Associated University Presses, 1981), p. 166.

25. See Jürgen Siebke, *Die Automobilnachfrage* (Cologne: Westdeutscher Verlag, 1963), pp. 79–81.

26. See Bundesminister für Verkehr (Ed.), *Verkehr in Zahlen 1972* (Hamburg: Deutscher Verkehrsverlag, 1973), pp. 28–29.

27. Angus Maddison, *The World Economy in the 20th Century* (Paris: OECD, 1989), p. 67.

28. *Statistisches Jahrbuch für die Bundesrepublik Deutschland 1952* [Statistical Yearbook of the Federal Republic of Germany, 1952] (Stuttgart: Kohlhammer, 1952), p. 243; *Statistisches Jahrbuch für die Bundesrepublik Deutschland 1966* (Stuttgart: Kohlhammer, 1966), p. 327.

29. This section is based partly on results of my project funded by the Deutsche Forschungsgemeinschaft (DFG), "Auswirkungen des Weltmarktes auf die Wirtschaft beider deutschen Staaten," published in the First Fuji Conference Series. See Werner Abelshauser, "Two kinds of Fordism: On the differing roles of the automobile industry in the development of the two German states," in Haruhito Shiomi and Kazuo Wada (Eds.), *Fordism Transformed: The Development of Production Methods in the Automobile Industry* (Oxford, England: Oxford University Press, 1995), pp. 269–296. See also note 3 in that publication.

30. Simon Reich, *The Fruits of Fascism: Postwar Prosperity in Historical Perspective* (Ithaca and London: Cornell University Press, 1990), p. 168.

31. Mira Wilkins and Frank Ernest Hill, *American Business Abroad: Ford on Six Continents* (Detroit: Wayne State University Press, 1964), p. 391.

32. Ibid.

33. Calculations based on data in Volker Wellhöner, *"Wirtschaftswunder" – Weltmarkt – westdeutscher Fordismus: Der Fall Volkswagen* (Münster: Dampfboot, 1996), Appendix, Table 5.3.

34. Deutsche Bundesbank, *Deutsches Geld und Bankwesen in Zahlen 1876–1975* (Frankfurt am Main: Fritz Knapp, 1976), p. 7.

35. Verband der Automobilindustrie (Ed.), *Geschäftsbericht für das Jahr 1961/62* [Annual report, 1961–1962] (Frankfurt am Main: VDA, 1962), p. 3.

36. See Achim Dieckmann, "Die Rolle der Automobilindustrie im wirtschaftlichen Wachstumsprozeß," in Verband der Automobilindustrie (Ed.), *Automobiltechnischer Fortschritt und wirtschaftliches Wachstum* (Frankfurt am Main: VDA, 1970), p. 101.

37. Wellhöner, *"Wirtschaftswunder,"* p. 112.

38. Ibid., pp. 113–114.

39. See Henry Ford (in collaboration with Samuel Crowther), *Moving Forward* (Garden City, NY: Doubleday, Doran & Company, 1930), ch. 9.

40. See Michael J. Piore and Charles F. Sabel, *The Second Industrial Divide: Possibilities for Prosperity* (New York: Basic Books, 1984), chs. 7 and 8.

41. On the divergence between the practices in Great Britain and the United States, see William Lazonick, *Competitive Advantage on the Shop Floor* (Cambridge, MA: Harvard University Press, 1990).

42. Ibid., p. 162.

43. Heinrich Nordhoff, *Reden und Aufsätze. Zeugnisse einer Ära* (Düsseldorf: Econ, 1992), p. 317.

44. Verband Automobilindustrie (VDA), *Geschäftsbericht, 1961/62* (Frankfurt am Main: VDA, 1962), p. 15; idem, *Geschäftsbericht, 1959/60* (Frankfurt am Main: VDA, 1960), p. 79.

45. The Volkswagen factory's presence on the margins of the world market is described in Wellhöner, *"Wirtschaftswunder,"* pp. 211–215.

46. Ibid., pp. 217–218.

47. Hans Matthöfer, Bericht über die Teilnahme am EPA-Programm PIO 07-43-175-60043 "Automation in Handel und Industrie," April 4, 1957, IG Metallarchiv im Archiv der sozialen Demokratie, IG Metall Vorstand, W 255.

48. See Piore and Sabel, *Industrial Divide*, ch. 7; Horst Kern and Michael Schumann, *Das Ende der Arbeitsteilung? Rationalisierung in der industriellen Produktion: Bestandsaufnahme, Trendbestimmung* (Munich: Beck, 1984).

49. *Frankfurter Allgemeine Zeitung*, 11 May 1998, p. 13.

50. See particularly Gerschenkron, "Economic backwardness."

51. Goetz Briefs, "Der wirtschaftliche Wert der Sozialpolitik," in Gesellschaft für Soziale Reform (Ed.), *Die Reform des Schlichtungswesens—Der wirtschaftliche Wert der Sozialpolitik: Bericht über die Verhandlungen der XI. Generalversammlung der Gesellschaft für soziale Reform in Mannheim am 24. und 25. Oktober 1929*, Schriften der Gesellschaft für Soziale Reform, vol. 83 (Jena: Gustav Fischer, 1930), p. 147.

52. Jeffrey A. Johnson, "The power of synthesis," in Werner Abelshauser (Ed.), *German Industry and Global Enterprise—BASF: The History of a Company* (Cambridge, England: Cambridge University Press, 2004), pp. 146–147.

53. Gerhard A. Ritter and Klaus Tenfelde, *Arbeiter im Deutschen Kaiserreich 1871 bis 1914* (Bonn: Dietz, 1992), pp. 422–424.

54. Werner Abelshauser, *Der Ruhrkohlenbergbau seit 1945. Wiederaufbau, Krise, Anpassung* (Munich: Beck, 1984), chap. 2.

55. Gloria Müller, *Mitbestimmung in der Nachkriegszeit. Britische Besatzungsmacht, Unternehmer, Gewerkschaften* (Düsseldorfer Schriften zur Neueren Landesgeschichte, vol. 21) (Düsseldorf: Schwann, 1987); idem, *Strukturwandel und Arbeitnehmerrechte. Die wirtschaftliche Mitbestimmung in der Eisen- und Stahlindustrie 1945–1975* (Düsseldorfer Schriften zur Neueren Landesgeschichte: vol. 31) (Essen: Klartext, 1991); Norbert Ranft, *Vom Objekt zum Subjekt* (Cologne: Bund, 1988); Werner Abelshauser, "Soziale Marktwirtschaft in Minden-Lübbecke: Der Arbeitgeber-Verband seit 1945," in W. Abelshauser (Ed.), *Die etwas andere Industrialisierung. Studien zur Wirtschaftsgeschichte des Minden-Lübbecker Landes im 19. und 20. Jahrhundert* (Essen: Klartext, 1999), pp. 269–293.

56. Barry Hirsch, John T. Addison, and Joachim Genosko, *Eine ökonomische Analyse der Gewerkschaften* (Regensburg: Transfer, 1990).

57. Lazonick, *Competitive Advantage*, pp. 310–312.

58. Abelshauser, *Staat*, pp. 9–58.

59. Martin Fiedler, "Betriebliche Sozialpolitik in der Zwischenkriegszeit. Wege der Interpretation und Probleme der Forschung im deutsch-französischen Vergleich," in *Geschichte und Gesellschaft*, 22 (1996), p. 370.

60. John J. Wallis and D.C. North, "Measuring the transaction sector in the American economy, 1870–1970," in Stanley L. Engerman and Robert E. Gallman (Eds.), *Long-Term Factors in American Economic Growth* (Chicago: Chicago University Press, 1986), pp. 95–161.

61. See Fukuyama, *Trust*, chap. 3.

62. See, for example, Fukuyama, *Trust*; Albert, *Capitalisme*, who stresses the "social superiority of the Rhine model"; and Soskice, "Globalisierung," who believes that the German "production regime" has retained its superiority on important markets under the conditions of globalization, too. This viewpoint was emphasized earlier by Andrew Shonfield as well in *Modern Capitalism: The Changing Balance of Public and Private Power* (Oxford, England: Oxford University Press, 1965).

63. Based on functional classification, recent calculations of the German economy's nonmaterial sector show that persons working in nonmaterial production (the tertiary sector) account for 75 percent of all employment (a figure that tends to reflect their percentage of value added in the economy as a whole). By contrast, only about 22 percent of all gainfully employed persons are engaged in material production (the industrial sector). See the *DIW-Wochenbericht*, 35 (1998).

64. The term comes from New Institutional Economics and was coined by Oliver E. Williamson in his book *The Economic Institutions of Capitalism: Firms, Markets, Relational Contracting* (New York: The Free Press, 1985), pp. 52–56.

65. See the contributions in Wolfgang Streeck and Norbert Kluge (Eds.), *Mitbestimmung*.

66. Wilhelm Roscher, *Grundlagen der Nationalökonomie*, 4th ed. (Stuttgart: Cotta, 1892), §42.

67. Adolph Wagner, *Die Ordnung des österreichischen Staatshaushalts, mit besonderer Berücksichtigung auf den Ausgabeetat und die Staatsschuld* (Vienna: Christian Bandstätter, 1984), p. 31. (Original work published 1863)

68. Theodor Mommsen, *Reden und Aufsätze* (Berlin: Weidmann, 1905), p. 209; Adolf von Harnack, "Vom Großbetrieb der Wissenschaft," *Preußische Jahrbücher*, 119 (1905), 193–201.

69. See Kurt Tucholsky's brilliant 1931 satire, "Wallenstein und die Interessenten," in Fritz J. Raddatz (Ed.), *Ausgewählte Werke*, vol. 2 (Reinbek bei Hamburg: Rowohlt, 1965), pp. 207–212.

70. Rudolf Hilferding, "Die Aufgaben der Sozialdemokratie in der Republik," in *Protokoll der Verhandlungen des sozialdemokratischen Parteitages 1927 in Kiel* (Berlin: Dietz, 1927), p. 168.

71. Ibid., p. 169.

72. Walter Eucken, "Staatliche Strukturwandlungen und die Krisis des Kapitalismus," *Weltwirtschaftliches Archiv* 36 (1932), p. 307.

73. Ibid, p. 315.

74. Alexander Rüstow, "Aussprache," in Franz Boese (Ed.), *Schriften des Vereins für Sozialpolitik: vol. 187. Deutschland und die Weltkrise, Verhandlungen des Vereins für Sozialpolitik in Dresden 1932* (Munich: Duncker & Humblot, 1932), pp. 64–65.

75. Ibid., p. 69.

IV. THE GERMAN ROAD TO THE TWENTY-FIRST CENTURY

Notes for this section begin on page 146.

1. Many Roads Lead to Rome

One result of this study is already clear: the search for the reasons for the durability of the German production regime in the previous one hundred years must begin in the late nineteenth century. The institutions that determined the "German path" in the twentieth century and that continue to inform institutional and, in particular, organizational change were shaped under the empire. The course staked out becomes even clearer when compared to the developmental lines of neighboring national economies, whose economic patterns of organization were formed against a different cultural background. Great Britain and the United States are of special interest in this respect. The British economy did not follow Germany's postindustrial transition in the late nineteenth century, whereas the American production regime initially had parallels with the German model but then increasingly diverged from it after 1900.

Germany and England developed quite different abilities and patterns in keeping with their own institutional conditions in order to prepare their economies for the pressing tasks of the twentieth century. In Great Britain, where the share of production accounted for by the tertiary sector had pulled even with that of the industrial sector by the turn of the century,[1] the modern service sector emerged as a vehicle for new economic objectives and as a guarantor of international competitiveness. Germany, by contrast, steadily pressed ahead with New Industry's expansion, which had begun around 1900. The share of value creation accounted for by New Industries' production of material goods has been superficial and degressive ever since, and the significance the German economy's "classical" tertiary sector remained comparatively small, not exceeding industry's share of production until the 1970s. Great Britain took a different direction. Although the relative weights there, too, gradually shifted toward scientific and technical education in the 1920s, the entry to New Industries was "hesitant, clumsy, and costly."[2] There can be no doubt that the British ability to benefit economically from new knowledge as a productive resource fell behind that of Germany, the United States, and a few other "industrialized countries" or was confined to relatively narrow areas of the tertiary sector, such as financial services. The causes are evidently not to be sought in the relative lack of access to knowledge as a "production factor" but rather in the obstacles to the new institutional and organizational wherewithal that would have helped make such knowledge available to the economy.

In historiographical terms, the causes of these obstacles are well known. The strong inclination toward capital export and direct investments abroad did not promote the development of New Industries within the country. Precisely the opposite situation pertained in Germany, where opportunities to acquire foreign holdings, make direct investments, and develop multinational companies were harder to come by than in England. Restrictions thereon strengthened domestic capital formation, particularly since Germany's all-purpose banks were willing to take on long-term commitments to that end and offered better conditions than did the British system of functional separation in the financial services sector. These differences in production regimes still exist today, for the stock exchange is of more consequence in the capital market in Britain than in Germany. In the early 1990s, it attracted capital totaling around 125 percent of Britain's gross national product; the corresponding figure in Germany was only 25 percent.[3] Granted, exceptions to the British principle of competition during the twentieth century have numbered as many as those to Germany's principle of regulated competition, but the respective underlying institutional arrangements are still clearly distinguishable from one another.

Comparison with the United States reveals a paradox. Although one may justifiably regard the twentieth century in many ways as the century of "Americanization," the divergence between the German and U.S. production systems is wider now than it was a hundred years ago (see Table 3). German economic practice would be all but inconceivable without the steady flow of new and innovative methods from the United States. Many "imports" from the United States, such as Taylorism, Fordism, the divisional structure of corporate organization, new management methods, and business practices like market research, marketing, and sales promotion, altered everyday business, as did substantial direct investment, which very often opened the door to the "Americanization" of the German economy. The triumphant march of these innovations usually also bequeathed Germany daily behavioral patterns that were usually welcomed by German entrepreneurs and managers. Admittedly, American influence came in waves—but Europe also had an impact on America. Before 1914 the balance of mutual enrichment may still quite possibly have been even. It clearly tipped in favor of the United States during the interwar period.

In the first phase of globalization, major German and American companies of New Industries were among the pioneers of world economic interdependence. AEG (founded in 1883) and Siemens AG, the flagships of the German electrical engineering industry, accounted for an estimated one third of the world production on their markets in 1913. At the turn of the twentieth century,

AEG had thirty-seven branch offices in European countries and thirty-eight overseas.[4] Even more impressive was the German chemical industry's focus on exports, an orientation that corresponded with overt reticence about building production facilities abroad unless customs and patent regulations required it. Until World War I, German companies dominated even the American market in electrochemical production and organic chemistry.[5] Both branches of industry were noted for reciprocal technology transfer between German and American companies. The two largest American chemical companies before 1945, Du Pont Company and Allied Chemical & Dye Corporation (or their founding companies), had worked with German patents even before 1914. AEG owed its rise to the rights to use Thomas Edison's inventions, which also laid the cornerstone for the ascent of the American company General Electric. The close relations between General Electric and AEG were formalized in 1903 with a contract on the exchange of patents and the partitioning of the world market. Transnational cooperation, capital links, and diffusion of technology between sizable German and American companies of New Industries also gave the world economy a new dimension. Despite this parallel development and similar ones presaging the upheaval of the economy's institutional framework in both countries at about the same time, the diverging elements of the social systems of production clearly prevailed (see Table 2).

Until well into the Third Reich, German political leaders, the business elite, and the broad public were fascinated by the U.S. economy because it represented the state of development that the German economy aspired to but could not achieve for political reasons and because of foreign trade policy. Since 1927, however, IG Farben had managed to cultivate close and lucrative business relations with Standard Oil of New Jersey (later Esso), one of the world's biggest companies.[6] Ironically, the process for making synthetic fuel—hydrogenation, which eventually sidelined IG Farben politically and economically in the 1930s—was the one that persuaded the American oil multinational to cooperate with the German trust on the construction of expansive pilot plants in the United States and a joint use of licenses. In the early 1930s, the technological strengths of IG Farben enabled it to regain prominence in international business, a status manifested in the Company for International Hydrogenation Patents, in which Esso, Imperial Chemical Industries (ICI), and Royal Dutch Shell participated. It was thus not any lack of innovativeness and active technology transfer from which the German chemical industry suffered in the 1940s. It was instead the long-term impacts of flawed business decision-making that ultimately doomed the sector to complete dependence on the Nazi regime and its policy of autarchy. In 1930, still before the worst of the Great Depression, the United States was the first of the main economic powers to turn its back on the world market. Digging in behind the walls of the Smoot-Hawley Tariff Act, the country staked its economic survival completely on its huge domestic market.

With the Marshall Plan after World War II, the United States once again became a mecca for German entrepreneurs and managers. At almost the same time, the United States registered increased immigration of German engineers and scientists—a brain drain from central Europe—along with a flood of technical and scientific know-how that an advance guard of German émigrés had heralded.[7] Although old capital links were restored and expanded soon after the war in many cases, the first wave of American direct investment did not reach Germany until the late 1950s. After the convertibility of the currency was guaranteed and West Germany's role in Europe seemed to have been clarified with the Treaties of Rome, the American challenge hit the Germans and the other Europeans as a shock.[8] A third industrial world power, after the United States and the Soviet Union, appeared on the horizon: the bases of U.S. multinational companies in Europe. Within only a few generations, the European powers faced the threatening possibility of losing their international influence along with this war without weapons and arms.[9] A culture clash loomed but did not deter the German economy from its course. Although no significant corporation went without the assistance of American consultants in the effort to adapt its structures to U.S. standards, this practice had not yet left any perceptible traces in the rules shaping corporate production regimes. With the fall of the dollar and the Fordist production regime, the appeal of the American economy even subsided temporarily in the 1970s, prompting American experts, too, to assess the future of the German economy positively because of its special institutional features.[10] But those days were long before the U.S. economy's resurgence in the 1990s and its subsequent consistently high performance resulting from the liberalization of the capital markets and the advent of the New Economy.

The transfer of behavioral patterns and values did not necessarily impel institutional (let alone organizational) change in the German economy, although "American" patterns of thought and behavior were willingly taken on. As an instrument of economic analysis, the concept of institutions should not be automatically equated with the thinking and behavior pervading an economy. In this context institutions are instead voluntarily chosen constraints on economic action. They are, as it were, rules of the game intended to simplify and stabilize what happens on the market and to minimize the costs of acquiring information and managing transaction costs. Although institutional change is partly determined by individual behaviors and shifts therein, it is keyed primarily to the cost-benefit ratios expected of possible institutional changes. In addition to economies of scale, the internalization of external effects, the reduction of risk, the redistribution of income, and profits gained by lowering transaction costs,[11] such triggers of institutional change include all changes that give the actors comparative institutional cost advantages in market competition. Such expectations are not general in nature; they always have to do with specific product markets clearly offering the prospect of comparative institutional cost advantages.

This background helps one understand the endurance of the basic institutional framework in Germany throughout the twentieth century. Since the end of the first phase of globalization, when the world economy futilely hoped to regain its dynamism after World War I, the markets that held promise for the German economy lay neither in the sale of highly innovative products nor in assembly-line production of batch goods. There was little capital for innovative new developments and insufficient demand for a "Fordist" production regime. The markets for diversified quality products became much more important, for that was where the German economy could fully exploit the strength it still had. Doing so successfully depended crucially on the use of mature, established technologies by a core of highly skilled workers and on high responsiveness to customers, which requires the ability to adapt to the customer's special wishes and to offer long-term service.[12] Prerequisites for attaining this goal, such as farsighted business strategies and decisions and intercompany cooperation, which had begun to include the employees as well before World War I, were strengthened and expanded because they went a long way to satisfying market needs for a reliable supply of diversified quality products (see Tables 2 and 3). It is no wonder that American values, institutions, and forms of organization were esteemed and admired by German companies but neither widely adopted in Germany[13] nor taken as catalysts for reorganizing the country's own production regime. Quite the contrary, the divergence between the two production regimes continued to widen.

Other, no less popular conjectures about the secular causes of institutional change must likewise be measured against the staying power of the German production regime. Mancur Olson's thesis is no exception. Olson asserts that, in the "losing states," the outcome of World War II broke up the social rigidities that had accumulated in long phases of stability that tended to paralyze interest intermediation. In his view, these countries thereby regained something that was blocked in the "winning states"—the ability to pursue the efficient and innovative reorganization of their social systems of production and, hence, to foster economic growth and technological progress.[14] But even this attempt to explain the numerous "economic miracles" of the long 1950s in terms of institutional change has limits, particularly when it comes to the prime example itself, Germany. The effect studied by Olson unmistakably helped remove the slag from discrete parts of the German production regime, such as union organization and the system of trade associations. It also did go some way to informalizing the cooperative structure of the German economy, especially the cartels, which still called the tune in German industry. In fact, their bureaucratic unwieldiness had become so notorious that even their advocates welcomed a loosening of cartel control. This foray, however, did not stop a return to the coordinated rules of economic activity, which the victorious powers had initially suspended (see Table 1). To the extent that sclerotic inflexibility in Germany's social system of production was reduced, the effect identified by Olson helps account for the longevity of the German production regime, which in many respects emerged from the country's collapse in 1945 leaner and more efficient than it had been.

2. Anachronisms of the "Economic Miracle"

The German economy thwarted most of the interventions attempted by the occupation powers and experienced the economic miracle of the long 1950s with a social system of production that essentially kept to the lines set out earlier in the century. This preference for established structures derives partly from the German economy's extraordinary success on product markets with proven technologies and highly diversified quality products, though it does have weaknesses against the market leader in each of a few highly innovative product areas. Recall, too, that the German economy's late nineteenth-century institutional framework had been conceived of as a reply to the trends toward the internationalization of the markets and the production process's ever greater reliance on scientific methods and theory. It had little catching up to do.

At the outset of the economic miracle, the West German economy had an attractive production regime, albeit basically an old one. This description also applies to those components that underwent a certain degree of institutionalization and formalization after 1945, as industrial relations did. In Germany, the introduction of workers' participation resumed something that well predated the years from 1947 to 1952: the trend toward seeking a specifically German answer to the agency problem and, hence, toward addressing the asymmetrical knowledge distribution typical of nonmaterial production in companies. But the concept of path dependency, no matter how flexibly applied, does not clarify everything. The critical point is the longevity of the incentive structures that have gone on determining the direction of institutional change since 1945 just as in previous periods. It has as much bearing on the German economy's market positions as it does on the necessity of tapping into the accumulated "capital" of German corporate culture for solving new problems.

The reconstruction period after World War II did little to alter the incentives for institutional change in the German economy during the long 1950s. This lack of encouragement may largely explain why it was not until relatively late that the economy had to adapt to the pressure exerted by market global-ization and the primacy of scientific methods and theory in production. The German production regime has always been prepared for both challenges, so its chances of meeting both are not hopeless. The public's only vague aware-ness of the problem since the oil-price shocks of the 1970s initially led to con-frontation with the prevailing doctrine of economic policy. Under the Grand Coalition (1966–1969), the social market economy of the long 1950s proved to be surprisingly flexible, taking a latter-day model of Keynesian-like coun-tercyclical fiscal and budget policy under its wing. The economy has been tied to clearly defined objectives ever since. "Growthmanship," the willingness and ability to plan economic expansion, was as much a part of it as the main-tenance of the macroeconomic balance and the assured survival of the welfare state. International cyclical fluctuations, however, quickly made it clear that equilibrium within the magic Keynesian triangle of objectives (full employ-ment, currency stability, and foreign-trade balance) could be neither legis-lated nor achieved through "concerted actions" patterned on corporatist interest mediation.

The overt inability of government economic policy to cope with the mounting problems of the labor market have therefore made neoliberal recipes seem more appealing again since the 1980s. A return to full employment was expected from supply-side economics, not from the management of demand. The state seemed ready to confine itself to guaranteeing stable monetary con-ditions and a favorable framework for investors and to reinvest business with the responsibility for the results of economic activity—though Germany seemed less eager to do so than countries with economic cultures of the Anglo-Saxon type. The experience of the last one hundred years casts doubt on whether this renewed shift in the paradigm of economic policy can solve the problem. Instead, it is necessary to wean government economic policy from its industrial orientation and give it firm institutional foundations on which to meet postindustrial needs through production-related design of the social and economic system on the part of the state. That kind of policy is not without models in the twentieth century, but the experience with them is overlain with mental associations rooted deep in the past of industrial societies. Mass unem-ployment appears to be the outcome of growing incompatibility that pits gov-ernment economic policy's abiding, publicly sanctioned commitment to the vision of industrialized society against a new reality where nonmaterial, postindustrial production accounts for 75 percent of employment and macro-economic value creation in Germany (German Institute for Economic Research). Although Germany was a pioneer of globalization and the primacy of scientific knowledge and methods in production before 1914, this disruption in the sense of direction in economic policy is especially pronounced in Germany as compared to other postindustrial nations. It owes to numerous set-backs of secular economic development that were the legacy of the politicoeconomic oscillation between crisis and reconstruction so typical of the twentieth century in Germany.

Since the late nineteenth century, the German economy's internal clock has marked time according to postindustrial forces driving nonmaterial production processes. However, the visible hands pointing to economic activity in the Weimar Republic, the Third Reich, and the postwar reconstruction period stopped on the industrial part of the dial in order to accommodate the needs of the catch-up processes. However, in the postwar and postdepression periods, economic policy long remained captive to this contradiction.

This anachronism of the economic paradigm was by no means overcome with the end of the reconstruction era. Even after the long 1950s, German economic policy frequently revolved around alleged imperatives of industrial economic development, with planners making decisions that further delayed the country's return as a vanguard of postindustrial development. Examples are easy to find. One of the most enduringly successful course corrections in these circumstances was the mass recruitment of unskilled foreign workers for the rising sector of Fordist mass production at the same time that the influx of well-trained labor from the German Democratic Republic ended with the construction of the Berlin wall.

The labor migrants arriving after 1961, however, differed not only in their actual skills from those who had already streamed into West Germany from central and eastern Germany but also in the severe social and cultural limitations on their potential adaptation to new occupations. The "guest workers" of the 1960s and 1970s were more promising for meeting the needs of industrial mass production based on simple skills than for helping restore the German economy to the superior position it once held within postindustrial development. The obvious presumption is that the availability of a seemingly limitless reservoir of what private business saw as relatively cheap labor retarded the use of nonmaterial production factors for streamlining production processes in every sector of the German economy. In this sense, Germany especially lagged behind rivals such as Japan, which did not use the opportunity to admit foreign workers, or the United States, which carefully screened them for certain skills. Of these two alternatives, the latter—organizing a brain drain benefiting the nonmaterial sector of the German economy—was far more difficult, if not impossible, because of legal, social, and cultural problems created by the migration of industrial workers and intensified by the vortex of peculiarities in asylum law.

If opening the labor market in the 1960s helped keep agriculture and old industries afloat, German economic policy-makers in both parts of the country succumbed to the illusion of their industrial vision and in many cases decided to preserve unprofitable sectors directly by means of government subsidies. Coal mining is a classical example of this process. Under the Grand Coalition, the government turned around coal mining in the Ruhr District in

1968 after a severe ten-year crisis in sales. It did so by consolidating the many mining companies there into a single enterprise, Ruhrkohle AG, and then working with all the participating interest groups to ensure the industry's systematic return to a viable size. This concerted action was expected to preserve competitive mining operations in the interest of the economy as a whole, relieve public budgets and social security in the medium term, and give the Rhine and Ruhr regions time to open up for economic structural change. The great political and financial effort entailed seemed to offer a pattern for methods and directions of publicly supported structural change that was feasible far beyond mining. It appeared to point the way to the postindustrial economy. However, the oil crises of 1973 and 1979 dashed the plan because the entrenched forces of industrial society and the mining lobby took them as a welcome occasion for revising the economic policy targets. In the high-tech Germany in the 1970s and 1980s, a priority of German research and technology policy was not to expand communications technology but rather to secure the conventional supply of energy by advancing coal technology.

Regardless of doctrine, reorienting economic policy and plotting its position was plainly more difficult in Germany than elsewhere in Europe. Since at least the 1990s, this impasse has put the production regime itself in the limelight, exposing it more and more to criticism.

3. Strengths and Weaknesses of the German Production Regime

Two results are telling. First, the amazing continuity of the German economy's institutional and organizational framework in the twentieth century is readily explicable by the fact that the main challenges posed by current markets have run along the main lines of economic development in Germany since the late nineteenth century. This is as true of the overall economy's institutional context as it is of the sectorial production regimes that have stamped this framework as the New Economy from the outset. The macroeconomy's social system of production and the institutional foundations of New Industries were therefore aimed at meeting the twentieth century's two paramount challenges: market globalization and the increasing reliance on scientific methods and theory in production processes.

Second, the most influential sectors of German industry have always had wide latitude, enabling them to open up new markets and set themselves apart from the institutional context of the entire economy. Since the 1960s, for example, large chemical plants have pursued vastly different entrepreneurial strategies under the same production regime. Whereas Sanofi-Synthelabo Aventis (formerly Hoechst–Rhône-Poulenc) has undertaken forward integration to flee the chemical industry and open a future market for itself in pharmaceuticals, BASF AG in the field of basic chemicals has perfected high technology with which it can combine the principles of diversified quality work with those of standardized mass production on a world scale.[15] Moreover, the ranks of New Industries have key transnational companies that operate under very dissimilar conditions throughout the world and selectively exploit their various institutional differences and advantages in order to stay competitive on the global market. From this international comparative viewpoint, the specific merits of their production regime have always been attractive.

Of course, these companies can exercise more flexibility and adapt better to market conditions in cases where they can directly affect their institutional structure at their German sites than in the economy as a whole. This phenomenon is by no means new. For instance, the major German chemical companies have never depended on banks; they have always raised their venture capital on the capital market. All the notable transnational companies of New Industries were embedded early in the "capital-market capitalism" that was emerging in the late nineteenth century. The same is also true of the sectors that, unlike chemicals, traditionally granted the large banks a considerable role in the system of corporate financing. The recent challenge to the German production regime therefore does not stem as much from the significance of the capital markets per se, which has been growing since the end of the Bretton Woods system, as from institutional changes within capital-market capitalism. The conflict reflects the risks entailed if this functional system of the global economy places itself outside all the agencies of national and international control. Both developments threaten the substance of the New Economy in Germany because they question one of its basic principles—long-term perspective of business initiative—and jeopardize the independence of the companies integrated into the capital market. There are many indications that the shift from a stakeholder frame of mind (among small shareholders, too) to the emphasis on shareholder value, which in the United States has become the sole standard of performance by listed companies since the 1990s,[16] is incompatible with the rules of the coordinated market economy and severely restricts its scope of action. Few German companies of the New Economy have drawn the necessary conclusions from this fact. Few have followed F. Porsche AG in rejecting these innovations, which are alien to their corporate culture.

Imitating other models of American management culture seems less problematic. Overseas advice to adjust the rules of corporate governance in favor of a strong CEO miss the mark because most companies of the German New Economy adopted that practice long ago, contravening the spirit of the German Stock Corporation Act without American conditions ensuing. Surprisingly, codetermination has come under less fire from the parties involved than public debate occasionally implies. In the late 1990s, its efficiency was certified by the Codetermination Commission, which the Bertelsmann Foundation and the Hans Böckler Foundation called upon to take stock of the practice carefully and to elaborate approaches by which to take it forward. The commission's members, recruited from all camps of the German economy, saw no reason for the unavoidable dispute over details "to allow the joint interest in a constructive further development of workers' participation to be forgotten."[17] The top representatives and experts of the German production regime unanimously held that wherever codetermination came into conflict with an enterprise's economic objectives, the cause lay not in the institution itself but rather in its local application. They called for the improvement, not the abolishment, of codetermination, urging that local processes be optimized and aligned with best practice as developed in the leading companies.

The present logjam blocking reform of the social system of production in Germany thus appears to be more a problem of policy than of corporate practice. However, experience at various levels of the German economy's institutional and organizational framework also shows that the intent of current discussion should not be to overhaul the economy's institutional context but rather to promote efficiency. The success that the production regime of New Industries is showing in the New Economy tends to argue in favor of reforming the system rather than replacing all of it, or even just supplanting parts of the social system of production with elements of a different, competing production regime. The practice of companies in the New Economy amply illustrates the direction that such reform could take. As shown in this book, the essentials that both the German production regime and German corporate culture bring to this task include, above all, accumulated capital of trust and the capacity for sociability. Both resources are required for structurally low transaction costs and, hence, for competitiveness on international markets. Popular wisdom holds that the importance of trust and social virtues as the source of prosperity in world society grows with globalization, of all conditions.[18] But if such cultural factors are increasingly determining the competitiveness of global economic actors, then Germany, precisely because of its traditional institutional framework, will be well equipped for the contest between economic cultures in the twenty-first century. The sustainability of the German economy will, of course, be decided on the world market.

Practical examples demonstrating the strengths and weaknesses of Germany's production regime and of the economy's organization are suggested by two standards for gauging economic success and competitiveness on product markets: the pattern of specialization reflected by patents granted, and the balance of trade in terms of surpluses and deficits. The former standard is a measure of the economy's ability to innovate, and it correlates with competitive position on the world market, though to varying degrees from one sector to the next. Surpluses and deficits in trade balance may serve as an index of a site's competitiveness.

The patents granted fully verify the generalization that the strengths of the German economic system lie especially in the markets for diversified quality production based on established technologies. A sample taken from 1989 through 1991 by the Fraunhofer Institute for Systems and Innovation Research in cooperation with its U.S. counterpart shows that German patents obviously tend to center on sectors whose technology has matured to the point that innovation can focus on specific economic applications (see Figure 2). These sectors are transport, machine-tool manufacturing, environmental technology, mechanics, engine-building, civil engineering and road construction, and thermal technology. The distribution of German patents conveys the impression that Germany's strengths begin where basic innovations become process innovations. By contrast, the German economy is weak in highly innovative sectors whose success requires a correspondingly flexible and risk-oriented production regime. They include information technology, semiconductor technology, optics, and biotechnology.

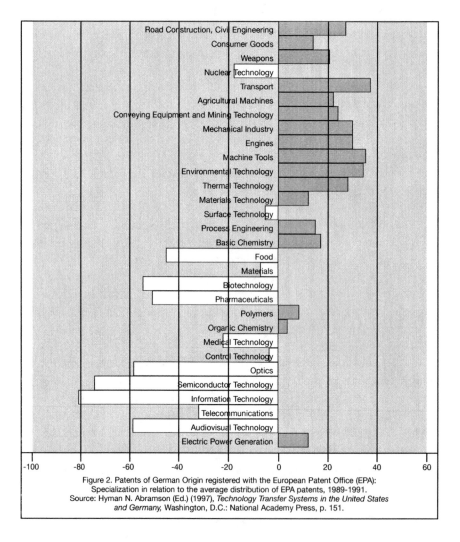

Figure 2. Patents of German Origin registered with the European Patent Office (EPA):
Specialization in relation to the average distribution of EPA patents, 1989-1991.
Source: Hyman N. Abramson (Ed.) (1997), *Technology Transfer Systems in the United States and Germany*, Washington, D.C.: National Academy Press, p. 151.

The influence that the social system of production has on "patent production" clearly comes out in a comparison between the German and American patterns of patent distribution (see Figure 3). In the United States, the most promising potential for innovation lies in information technology, medical technology, biotechnology, pharmaceuticals, and nuclear technology—the very sectors where innovativeness is relatively weak in Germany. In the United States, conversely, the strength of the ability to innovate is underdeveloped where long-term corporate horizons or highly and broadly skilled labor is crucial. Superimposing the one pattern of distribution onto the other, one sees with striking clarity that the two production regimes complement each other almost completely in terms of their ability to innovate. The strengths of the one are the weaknesses of the other and vice versa. This picture has remained pretty much unaltered to this very day.[19]

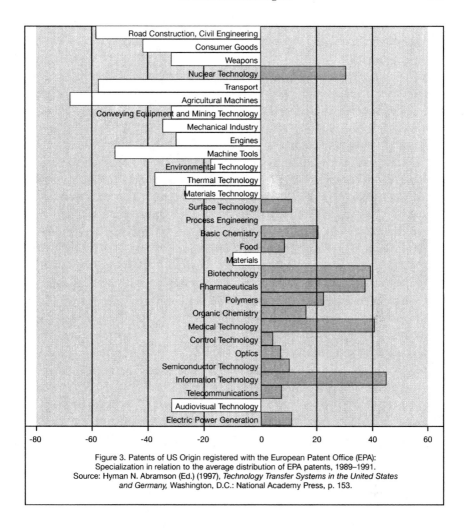

Figure 3. Patents of US Origin registered with the European Patent Office (EPA):
Specialization in relation to the average distribution of EPA patents, 1989–1991.
Source: Hyman N. Abramson (Ed.) (1997), *Technology Transfer Systems in the United States
and Germany,* Washington, D.C.: National Academy Press, p. 153.

Similarly, the strengths and weaknesses of the German social system of production can be read from the trade balance accounts. The most dynamic performance of Germany's export economy is in automotive manufacturing, machine manufacturing, and the chemical industry, whereas it conspicuously lags on the market for modern office machines and other components of computer processing. Although the German export economy, unlike the American or Japanese, is not the complete master on any segment of the world market, the breadth and depth of its international position is surprising. In 1985, for example, Germany's average share of world exports (10.6 percent) was exceeded by no fewer than 345 German industries in their respective fields of business.[20] The combined total exports from just seven of them accounted for more than 1 percent of all German exports that year. This breadth indicates that Germany's export economy pursues a strategy of differentiation centering on industries with a relatively high degree of specialization and high productivity. The nation therefore weathers competition and cyclical fluctuations especially well. This capacity currently shows up in the German export economy's ability to defend its position despite the significant rise in the number of competitors on the world market in the previous decade. Of course, Germany's continuous success with exports since the early 1950s is still closely linked to the comparative institutional cost advantages that the German economy enjoys on markets for diversified quality products.[21]

Machine manufacturing, a pivotal industry in every competitive export "cluster," is no exception. In 1985 Germany had more than forty-six internationally competitive lines of machine manufacturing; the United States, only seventeen. The opposite was true on the market for international services, where the management of large and complex systems counts as much as access to the skills of well-trained self-employed persons. The United States had forty-four such lines of business as opposed to Germany's seven. The numerical relations of the two countries' national sectors were even more unbalanced where the use of electronic components is escalating, as is the case on the market for office appliances and Telecom products. Fears that this gap could quickly widen have not been borne out. In fact, a market has developed in the manufacture of machines for products of the New Economy, whereby a disproportionately high increase in patent registrations has proven the innovativeness of the German machine-manufacturing industry.[22] The German economy appears to be catching up with the U.S. economy and seems to be pressing on with "innovative product modernization," albeit along different paths.[23] Not surprisingly, German companies have increased their concentration on technology, innovation, and a customer-friendly product design, with the inherent danger of overengineering. American companies aspire to price leadership more frequently than German companies do. No longer completely dominating electronic business, American companies have meanwhile allowed their German rivals to take the lead in applying methods linking computer-aided design, work planning, and production, although these CAD systems originated in American software laboratories of the aerospace industry.

Nevertheless, Germany's New Economy will have a problem if its success stays confined to product markets using established technologies and if it remains a weak competitor on highly innovative product markets, such as those for office machines and other components of computer processing. The cardinal question for the future then becomes whether the German production regime can keep proving its strength in the phase when basic innovations in a given product cycle move on to process innovations. Can it repeatedly come through when newly developed technologies reach the stage at which the main thing is to utilize them for specific economic purposes? If so, that is the point at which the German production regime could bring its comparative advantages fully into play. However, if the German economy steadily loses its ability to develop new product cycles on its own, it could eventually fail to keep up with shaping new product cycles. In the first case, the German production regime would be able to demonstrate its strengths again and again. Lingering weaknesses would then be all the easier to offset through compensatory strategies, such as direct foreign investment, in order to exploit different comparative institutional and material advantages.

In the second case, the overhaul of the German economy's institutional framework would have to be tackled seriously. Given the current discussion, however, the question would be whether the German production regime has really become obsolete or whether it needs internal systems reform in order to adapt it to new outward manifestations of developments to which it has long been oriented in principle. By contrast, the only response that seems out of the question is to replace individual parts of the system with "modules" alien to it. The discrete components of the system closely mesh with each other, intricacies that account for much of its success.[24] With numerous transnational companies, there are already clear signs of failure with entrepreneurial reform strategies based on concepts imported from the U.S. production regime. Having experienced an initial phase of unconditional adaptation to American practices of corporate governance, financing, or industrial relations, German multinationals are beginning to ponder whether precisely that change could be the cause of acute problems presently hitting them especially hard. The major German banks, a branch of the New Economy that has compelled this strategy of fleeing the portfolio of its own, long-standing sectorial culture, are verging on despair about their very survival. What has happened there could jeopardize the entire economy if it overextends its portfolio through selective reforms. Despite massive effort, the German banks have neither gained a footing in investment banking nor managed to straddle both cultures without neglecting their traditional core business. The economic and moral decline of Deutsche Bank is an instructive example. Change in the social system of production is therefore bound to encroach on the identity of German society more profoundly than most critics are aware when they call for thorough modernization. That kind of discontinuity would not be unprecedented in German economic history. The era of the German empire gives an idea of how a production regime (the liberal market economy) can be quickly replaced by another (the coordinated market economy) after a long-smoldering crisis. But it also illustrates the ordeals that a society may have to endure in the process.

Basically, however, there is no reason to doubt that the coordinated market economy can creatively adopt the new developments arising from the knowledge and information society. Evidence that it can take them on lies in Germany's own historical experience. There are also other examples bearing out the experience that a welfare state in which cooperative labor relations prevail and in which government policies shape much of the overall context in which business is conducted is quite able to stand up to the American model on its own ground. Finland's ascendance to global leadership as a supplier of IT in the 1990s verified the possibility of achieving a high level of technology and competitiveness from quite different points of departure and economic development.[25] The Scandinavians have not suffered the social inequality that the Californian model seems to foster, nor have they resorted to the authoritarian political means that Singapore and other southeast Asian "Tiger States" use to survive in the competition of the global new economy. On the contrary, the Scandinavians have succeeded in transforming the characteristics of their own social system of production into comparative competitive advantages. A union membership rate of 80 percent—as is the case with the workforce in Finland—need not contradict the inherent laws of the new economy. That degree of organization can instead guarantee the stability of labor relations, which facilitates flexibility in shaping venturesome business strategies on innovative markets. In return, the unions have the security of the welfare state and the advantages that a growing economy means for employment and wage policy. A comparatively high rate of taxes and levies is productive and politically tolerable as long as it provides all citizens an attractive level of welfare benefits, a high quality of life, and the infrastructure necessary for people and markets to perform well. The welfare state need not hinder the continued development of the new economy. It can open new markets, as shown by the Finnish example of linking health care and IT.

As similar as Finland and Germany are in the pattern underlying their respective social systems of production, they are just as different in another respect. Emerging in the 1990s from relative poverty and a state of absolute backwardness in IT, Finland joined the world's top ranks in that field. The country boasts a cluster of more than 3,000 IT businesses, with Nokia as a corporate icon—not to mention Linux, an originally Finnish open source operating system that is now challenging Windows. Germany, by contrast, lacks economic incentives for reforms, a problem resulting from satiation and a desire to maintain the status quo. But the country does have what it takes for reform.

Above all, the economic portfolio of Germany has to be throughly understood by the country's policy-makers. Veteran experience with markets and corporate or economic cultures are greater determinants of the economy's abilities and disabilities than brave decisions by policy-makers or economic elites are. Research on organizational behavior teaches that attempts to move against the grain of one's corporate culture can fail, and often have failed, when it means leaving an established portfolio so as to succeed on weaker markets. Since the 1990s, most German companies have therefore concentrated on their core business in order to optimize their strengths. This recommendation would suit the German social system of production with its powerful economic culture. Institutions that have taken shape over extended periods can be destroyed quickly, but it takes a long time to build new rules and economic structures— with no certainty that such a radical operation will succeed.

As long as the German innovation machine is not certifiably breathing its last, there is no meaningful alternative to trying to liberate it from decades of slag and to keep it compatible with new developments, including demographic ones. This perspective should direct the attention of reformers first to the erroneous decisions of the 1970s, which centered on the anachronistic industrial worldview rooted in the period of the economic miracle. There is not a moment to lose in adapting Germany's economic and social policy to postindustrial conditions. That adjustment is long overdue.

State intervention policy should begin at home, that is, with a redefinition of the government's role in the economy. Granted, the German innovation machine is inconceivable without its integration into the collective flow of goods attributable to government macroeconomic policies that set the overall context in which business is conducted. But a production regime designed for diversified quality work cannot function unless it has a barrier-free, operational training and research system providing for equal economic opportunity and for optimal use of available human capital. It is to this concern that the state must redirect its attention. Elite universities are not required in order to provide these essentials. The German innovation machine depends instead on high-quality broad education (though elite universities could not hurt once that quality is attained). The state must also promote top-flight research, too, which has long been among the institutional foundations of the innovativeness for which Germany's social system of production is known.

These elements of state production-related design of the social and economic system now test the behavior of the actors even more than the role of the state. Rhine capitalism will retain its attractiveness only if its actors know what to do to make the system work, if they want to do it, and if everything necessary is done so that they can. This "if" is where a two-track strategy of reforms must begin in order to liberate such frameworking from the anachronisms of the declining industrial economy and continually adapts the economy's institutional framework to the needs of postindustrial development.

The variety and density of the institutional landscape demand more sociability of the economic actors than ever before. The aim to ensure that the German economy retains its comparative institutional cost advantage on the markets for diversified quality products and thereby preserves the chance to assert its strengths and continue expanding. To achieve that goal its actors must demonstrate the will and ability to use the complex, entrenched network of rules, cooperative relations, and trust purposefully and to see it as a competitive advantage. The impetus to do so must come from the markets. From their economic logic it must elicit behavioral patterns that constitute a social system of production. These elemental capacities of the German economy to succeed at these tasks obviously still exist, for its worldwide competitiveness can hardly be doubted. The problem lies rather in the rise of particular interests that believe they are justified in resisting incorporation into a German social system of production *(Deutschland AG)*.

In particular, major companies operating as global players on the world market have the alternative of building solely on markets and hierarchies so as to increase flexibility and maximize short-term profit. The decision to withdraw from the corporative market economy is not rooted in any arbitrariness of the business community. The more the international capital market is dominated by rules that complicate long-term strategic thinking and interfere with corporate governance, the more German companies face a dilemma. Should they accept the new rules of the game and thereby risk breaking with their own corporate culture and losing their comparative institutional advantages on the world market? Or should they keep building their strengths by helping to ensure that Rhine capitalism can function—and by restoring it where necessary—even if they have to forfeit some of the advantages offered by the international capital market? Because these different strategies have economic consequences and profoundly affect people's ways of life, the choice between the options requires a fundamental political decision—especially since none of the alternative strategies can afford to dispense with the policy-making community as a resource. This context and the obligation to use property in the service of the public good (Basic Law, Article 14, paragraph 2) legitimately invests state policy with the organizational and regulatory task of keeping the actors aware of their role in and responsibility for the social system of production.

Since the end of the great antagonism between the economic systems in East and West, divergent cultural factors have conditioned the global economy more and more. That reality suggests a course of action focused on streamlining the institutional framework yet also retaining its characteristic features and emphasizing its competitiveness. A good deal of evidence refutes the notion that there is only one way to ensure long-term competitiveness on the world market. The path need not be that of homogeneous entrepreneurial "best practice" shaped by the neoclassical ideal of deregulated markets and unrestricted entrepreneurial prerogatives. History demonstrates that different market conditions demand different institutional responses on the supply side. Production regimes with dense institutional landscapes in which fixed rules have evolved, as in most European countries, need not be less competitive than U.S.-style national economies with weak institutions, which leave organization and controllability primarily up to markets and hierarchies. German economic policy at the dawn of the twenty-first century should therefore not be confined to imitating innovation regimes of successful competitors but rather should creatively expand the economy's own comparative institutional advantages.

Notes

1. Colin Clark, *The Conditions of Economic Progress* (London: MacMillan, 1940), p. 187.
2. Sidney Pollard, *The Development of the British Economy: 1914–1967* (London: Arnold, 1970), pp. 93–94.
3. William P. Kennedy, "Die Rezeption des deutschen Bankensystems in England. Vom belächelten „Unsinn" zum "Vorbild," in Hartmut Berghoff and Dieter Ziegler (Eds.), *Pioniere und Nachzügler? Vergleichende Studien zur Geschichte Großbritanniens und Deutschlands im Zeitalter der Industrialisierung.* Volume commemorating the 70th birthday of Sidney Pollard (Bochum: Brockmeyer, 1995), p. 99.
4. Peter Hertner, "Financial strategies and adaption to foreign markets: The German electrotechnical industry and its multinational activities, 1890s to 1939," in Alice Teichova, Maurice Leboyer, and Helga Nussbaum (Eds.), *Multinational Enterprise in Historical Perspective* (Cambridge, England: Cambridge University Press, 1986), pp. 145–159.
5. Alfred D. Chandler, *Scale and Scope: The Dynamics of Industrial Capitalism* (Cambridge, MA: Belknap, 1990), pp. 474–486.
6. Ray G. Stokes, "From the IG Farben fusion to BASF AG (1925–1952)," in Abelshauser, *BASF*, pp. 206–361; here, pp. 226–230.
7. See John Gimbel, *Science, Technology, and Reparations: Exploitation and Plunder in Postwar Germany* (Stanford, CA: Stanford University Press, 1990), and Matthias Judt and Burghard Ciesla (Eds.), *Technology Transfer out of Germany after 1945* (Amsterdam: harwood academic publishers, 1996).
8. See Jean-Jacques Servan-Schreiber, *The American Challenge*, Trans. Ronald Steel (London: Hamilton, 1968).
9. Ibid.
10. Herman Kahn and Michael Redepenning, *Die Zukunft Deutschlands. Niedergang oder neuer Aufstieg der Bundesrepublik* (Stuttgart: Poller, 1982).
11. Knut Borchardt, "Der 'Property Rights-Ansatz' in der Wirtschaftsgeschichte," in Jürgen Kocka (Ed.), *Theorien in der Praxis des Historikers. Forschungsbeispiele und ihre Diskussion* (Göttingen: Vandenhoek & Ruprecht, 1977), p. 151.
12. Streeck, "Diversified quality production," pp. 21–61.
13. Paul Erker, "'Amerikanisierung' der westdeutschen Wirtschaft? Stand und Perspektive der Forschung," in Konrad Jarausch and Hannes Siegrist (Eds.), *Amerikanisierung und Sowjetisierung in Deutschland 1945–1970* (Frankfurt am Main and New York: Campus, 1997). All things being equal, this point also applies to other European national economies. See Nick Tiratsoo and Jim Tomlinson, *Industrial Efficiency and State Intervention: Labour 1939–1951* (London: Routledge, 1993); Noel Whiteside and Robert Salais, *Governance, Industry and Labour Markets in Britain and France, 1930–1960: The Modernizing State* (London: Routledge, 1997); Jonathan Zeitlin, *Between Flexibility and Mass Production: Strategy, Debate and Industrial Reorganization in British Engineering, 1830–1990* (Oxford, England: Oxford University Press, 1997).
14. Mancur Olson, *The Rise and Decline of Nations: Economic Growth, Stagflation, and Social Rigidities* (New Haven, CT: Yale University Press, 1982).
15. As recent developments have shown, however, each of IG Farben's successor companies had only one alternative strategy that was favorable in the long run. See Abelshauser, *BASF*, ch. 9.
16. Alfred Rappaport, *Creating Shareholder Value: The New Standard for Business Performance* (New York: The Free Press, 1986).
17. Bertelsmann Stiftung and Hans-Böckler-Stiftung (Eds.), *Mitbestimmung und neue Unternehmenskulturen – Bilanz und Perspektiven. Bericht der Mitbestimmungskommission* (Gütersloh: Bertelsmann Stiftung, 1998), p. 119.
18. Fukuyama, *Trust*.

19. Deutsches Patent- und Markenamt [German Patent and Trademark Office], *Jahresbericht 2001* [Annual Report] (Munich: Heymann, 2002), pp. 20–21.
20. Porter, *Competitive Advantage*, p. 356. The breakdown of the industries follows the United Nations' Standard International Trade Classification (SITC).
21. Porter, *Competitive Advantage*; Linda von Delhaes-Günther, *Erfolgsfaktoren des westdeutschen Exports in den 1950er u. 1960er Jahren* (Dortmund: Gesellschaft für Westfälische Wirtschaftsgeschichte, 2003).
22. IFO-Institut für Wirtschaftsforschung, "Der mittelständische Maschinenbau am Standort Deutschland – Chancen und Risiken im Zeitalter der Globalisierung und 'New Economy'," Munich, October 2001.
23. See Jürgen Wengel and Gunter Lay, "Deutschland und die USA auf verschiedenen Wegen. Konzepte der Produktionsmodernisierung im Vergleich" [Entire issue], Fraunhofer ISI, *Mitteilungen aus der Produktionsinnovationserhebung*, 23 (September 2001).
24. Soskice, "Globalisierung," pp. 207–208.
25. See Manuel Castells and Pekka Himanen, *The Information Society and the Welfare State: The Finnish Model* (Oxford, England: Oxford University Press, 2002).

Postscript

BY JÖRN RÜSEN

This book is based on the lecture entitled "Culture Clash: Historical Perspectives on the Sustainability of the German Economy," which Werner Abelshauser delivered in October 2002 as part of the Pott Lecture Series on Technology, Business, and Culture. The Pott lectures are organized by the Kulturwissenschaftliches Institut in Essen to address a broad audience on issues and viewpoints in the humanities. The tradition of having prominent thinkers present syntheses of their research not only to specialists but to the interested lay public as well is not yet highly developed in Germany. But because the sciences in general, and the humanities in particular, account for much of the culture of the society in which they are institutionalized (and funded), they live also from repeatedly examining and substantiating their role in the culture of their times.

There are areas of science—especially in the natural sciences, engineering, medicine, and some of the social sciences such as economics and law—whose social utility is so evident that it does not seem necessary to give them a second thought. Yet in those technical fields, too, research priorities and disciplinary preferences are becoming ever more closely linked with the needs and interests of society. The public attention they are attracting stems from that development and must be constantly attended to for the sake of research funding and the cultural prestige of experts.

With the practical utility of the natural sciences being so obvious, the imperative is that much greater for the cultural sciences to communicate to the public. Although no modern educational system would be conceivable without the cultural sciences, and although the knowledge they offer is constantly drawn upon, they are under greater pressure to justify themselves than the natural sciences are. It is all the more necessary to stress the overarching significance of the cultural sciences and to point out their universal relevance again and again.

The Kulturwissenschaftliches Institut in Essen has sought to do precisely that in various ways, including presentations, congresses, conferences, debates, and public lectures in the Anglo-Saxon tradition. The lectures exhibit the varied epistemological orientation and range of the contribution by the cultural sciences: the Krupp Lectures on History and Politics, the Essen Lectures on Philosophy, Culture, and Art, and the Pott Lectures on Technology, Business, and Culture.

The Pott lectures are intended to explain how technology and business are culturally conditioned, that each has its own instrumental logic always develops and emerges from specific contexts with specific cultural reason. "Cultural reason" means identifying the sense of human action and suffering in which the human being—in his subjectivity as the signifier and interpreter of his world and himself—expresses and explains. Of course, instrumental reason is also part of culture. Without it, without the ability to find and effectively use suitable means of realizing given objectives, humans could not accomplish their life tasks. But culture is always also more. It is also creative consideration of the ends themselves. And sense is the supreme criterion by which each end is set, contemplated, legitimated, critiqued, and negotiated.

The intention of the Pott lectures is to point out this inherent sense, the special cultural essence in technology and economic activity. These cultural elements are often overlooked or underestimated in their significance—to the detriment of technological and business. Held up to the light of attention, they can reveal their significance to all alert actors involved and thereby increase the opportunity for pertinent, effective, and argumentative inquiry into the sense *of* technology and the economy as the sense *in* technology and the economy. The opportunity also increases for knowledge from research in the humanities to strengthen that thinking.

Without patrons, lecture series of this kind are very difficult, if not impossible, to offer. The name of this series expresses the commitment of the Alfred and Cläre Pott Foundation to promote the efforts of the Kulturwissenschaftliches Institut to present the humanities as part of the culture in which we live. I thank the foundation, particularly Dr. Klaus Liesen and Dr. Ulrich Unger for their interest and support. Special gratitude goes to the author, Werner Abelshauser, for accepting the challenge of elucidating the link between technology, business, and culture in relation to a key topic and for elaborating his lecture into a small, readable book. Lastly, I thank the publisher, Marion Berghahn, for finding such a suitable form for the claim that cultural research has on public interest.

Select Bibliography

Abelshauser, Werner (1980), "Staat, Infrastruktur und interregionaler Wohlstandsausgleich im Preußen der Hochindustrialisierung," in Fritz Blaich (Ed.), *Staatliche Umverteilungspolitik in historischer Perspektive: Beiträge zur Entwicklung des Staatsinterventionismus in Deutschland und Österreich,* Schriften des Vereins für Socialpolitik, New Series, vol. 109, Berlin: Duncker & Humblot, pp. 9–58.

_____ (1984), "The first post-liberal nation: Stages in the development of modern corporatism in Germany," *European History Quarterly*, 14/3, 285–318.

_____ (1995), "Two kinds of Fordism: On the differing roles of the automobile industry in the development of the two German states," in Haruhito Shiomi and Kazuo Wada (Eds.), *Fordism Transformed: The Development of Production Methods in the Automobile Industry*, Oxford, England: Oxford University Press, pp. 269–296.

_____ (1998), "Germany: guns, butter, and economic miracles," in Mark Harrison (Ed.), *The economics of World War II: Six Great Powers in International Comparison,* Cambridge, England: Cambridge University Press, pp. 122–176.

_____ (2002), "Rüstungsschmiede der Nation? Der Kruppkonzern im Dritten Reich und in der Nachkriegszeit 1933 bis 1951," in Lothar Gall (Ed.), *Krupp im 20. Jahrhundert: Die Geschichte des Unternehmens vom Ersten Weltkrieg bis zur Gründung der Stiftung*, Berlin: Siedler, part III, pp. 267–472.

_____ (2004), *Deutsche Wirtschaftsgeschichte seit 1945*, Munich: C.H. Beck.

_____ (Ed.) (2004), *German Industry and Global Enterprise—BASF: The History of a Company* (David Antal and Anne Stokes, Trans.), New York and Cambridge, England : Cambridge University Press.

Albert, Michel (1991), *Capitalisme contre Capitalisme*, Paris: Edition du Seuil.

Amemiya, Akihiko (2005), *The Politics of Competitive Order. The Origins of Economic Policy Thought in Germany,* Tokyo: Nihon Keizai Hyoronska.

Ashley, William (1888), *An Introduction to English Economic History and Theory*, part I, London: Longman, Green & Co.

Barkin, Kenneth D. (1970), *The Controversy over German Industrialization 1890–1902*, Chicago: University of Chicago Press.

Bell, Daniel (1973), *The Coming of Post-Industrial Society: A Venture in Social Forecasting*, New York: Basic Books.

Berg, Maxine; Pat Hudson, and Michael Sonenscher (Eds.) (1983), *Manufacture in Town and Country before the Factory*, Cambridge, England: Cambridge University Press.

Berghahn, Volker R. (1986), *The Americanization of West German Industry, 1945–1973*, Leamington Spa, UK, New York: Berg.

_____ (1994), *Imperial Germany, 1871–1914: Economy, Society, Culture, and Politics*, Providence, RI: Berghahn Books.

_____ (1987), *Modern Germany: Society, Economy, and Politics in the Twentieth Century*, 2nd ed., Cambridge, England, New York: Cambridge University Press.

_____ and Detlef Karsten (1987), *Industrial Relations in West Germany*, New York: St. Martin's Press.

Bertelsmann Foundation and Hans-Böckler Foundation (Eds.) (1998), *Co-Determination and New Corporate Cultures – Survey and Perspectives: Report of the Co-Determination Commission*, Gütersloh: Verlag Bertelsmann Stiftung.

Blackbourn, David and Geoff Eley (1984), *The Peculiarities of German History: Bourgeois Society and Politics in Nineteenth-Century Germany*, Oxford, England: Oxford University Press.

Bluestone, Barry and Bennett Harrison (2000), *Growing Prosperity: The Battle for Growth with Equity in the 21st Century*, New York: The Century Foundation.

Borchardt, Knut (1977), "Der 'Property Rights-Ansatz' in der Wirtschaftsgeschichte," in Jürgen Kocka (Ed.), *Theorien in der Praxis des Historikers: Forschungsbeispiele und ihre Diskussion*, Göttingen: Vandenhoeck & Ruprecht, pp. 140–160.

_____ (2001), *Globalisierung in historischer Perspektive*, Bayerische Akademie der Wissenschaften, Philosophisch-historische Klasse—Sitzungsberichte, Heft 2, Munich: C.H. Beck.

Bordo, Michael D.; Barry Eichengreen; and Douglas A. Irwin (1999), "Is globalization today really different than globalization a hundred years ago?" NBER Working Paper Series 7195, Cambridge, MA.

Boserup, Ester (1981), *Population and Technological Change: A Study of Long-Term Trends*, Chicago: University of Chicago Press.

Bowen, Ralph H. (1947), *German Theories of the Corporative State*, New York and London: McGraw-Hill.

Burt, Roger (1995), "The transformation of non-ferrous metals industries in the 17th and 18th centuries," *Economic History Review*, 48, 23–45.

Calleo, David P. (1978), *The German Problem Reconsidered: Germany and the World Order, 1870 to the Present*, Cambridge, England, and New York: Cambridge University Press.

Cameron, Rondo (1982), "The Industrial Revolution: A misnomer," *The History Teacher*, 15, 377–384.

_____ (1985), "A new view of European industrialization," *Economic History Review* (2nd Series), 38, 1–23.

Castells, Manuel and Pekka Himanen (2002), *The Information Society and the Welfare State: The Finnish Model*, Oxford: Oxford University Press.

Chandler, Alfred D. (1990), *Scale and Scope: The Dynamics of Industrial Capitalism*, Cambridge, MA: Belknap.

Clark, Colin (1940), *The Conditions of Economic Progress*, London: MacMillan.

Cobbett's Parliamentary History of England (1807), vol. 2, London: Bagshaw.

Crafts, Nicholas F.R. (1985), *British economic growth during the Industrial Revolution*, Oxford, England: Oxford University Press.

_____ and C. Knick Harley (1992), "Output growth and the British industrial revolution: A restatement of the Crafts-Harley view," *Economic History Review* (2nd Series), 45, 703–730.

Cunningham, William (1915), *The Growth of English Industry and Commerce during the Early and Middle Ages* (5th ed.), Cambridge, England: Cambridge University Press. (Original work published 1882)

Delhaes-Günther, Linda von (2003), *Erfolgsfaktoren des westdeutschen Exports in den 1950er u. 1960er Jahren*, Dortmund: Gesellschaft für Westfälische Wirtschaftsgeschichte.

Deutsche Bundesbank (1976), *Deutsches Geld und Bankwesen in Zahlen 1876–1975*, Frankfurt am Main: Fritz Knapp.

Deutsches Patent- und Markenamt [German Patent and Trademark Office] (2002), *Jahresbericht 2001*, Munich: Heymann.

Drucker, Peter F. (1993), *Post-Capitalist Society*, New York: HarperBusiness.

Edelmann, Heidrun (1989), *Vom Luxusgut zum Gebrauchsgegenstand: Die Geschichte der Verbreitung von Personenkraftwagen in Deutschland*, Frankfurt am Main: Verband der Automobilindustrie (VDA).

Eley, Geoff (1978), "Capitalism and the Wilhelmine state: Industrial growth and political backwardness in recent German historiography, 1890–1918," *Historical Journal*, 21, 737–750.

Erker, Paul (1997), "'Amerikanisierung' der westdeutschen Wirtschaft? Stand und Perspektive der Forschung," in Konrad Jarausch and Hannes Siegrist (Eds.), *Amerikanisierung und Sowjetisierung in Deutschland 1945–1970*, Frankfurt am Main and New York: Campus, pp. 137–145.

Feldman, Gerald D. (1974), "Der deutsche organisierte Kapitalismus während der Kriegs- und Inflationsjahre 1914–1923," in Heinrich A. Winkler (Ed.), *Organisierter Kapitalismus*, Göttingen: Vandenhoeck & Ruprecht, pp. 150–171.

_____ (1977), *Iron and Steel in the German Inflation, 1916–23*, Princeton, NJ: Princeton University Press.

Feldman, Gerald D. (with Irmgard Steinisch) (1985), *Industrie und Gewerkschaften 1918–1924*, Stuttgart: Deutsche Verlagsgesellschaft.

Fischer, Wolfram (1964), *Unternehmerschaft, Selbstverwaltung und Staat*, Berlin: Duncker & Humblot.

Fischer, Wolfram; R. Marvin McInnis; and Jürgen Schneider (Eds.) (1986), *The Emergence of a World Economy, 1500–1914*, Wiesbaden: Steiner.

Ford, Henry (in collaboration with Samuel Crowther) (1930), *Moving Forward*, Garden City, NY: Doubleday, Doran & Company.

Foreman-Peck, John (1985), *A History of the World Economy: International Economic Relations since 1850*, Brighton: Harvester Press.

Fukuyama, Francis (1992), *The End of History*, New York: The Free Press.

_____ (1995), *Trust: The Social Virtues and the Creation of Prosperity*, New York: The Free Press.

Gerschenkron, Alexander (1952), "Economic backwardness in historical perspective," in Bert F. Hoselitz (Ed.), *The Progress of Underdeveloped Areas*, Chicago: Chicago University Press, pp. 3–29.

Gierke, Otto von (1954), *Das deutsche Genossenschaftsrecht*, vol. 1. Darmstadt: Wissenschaftliche Buchgesellschaft. (Original work published 1868)

Gimbel, John (1990), *Science, Technology, and Reparations: Exploitation and Plunder in Postwar Germany*, Stanford, CA: Stanford University Press.

Gross, Charles (1890), *The Gild Merchant* (2 vols.), Oxford, England: Oxford University Press.

Hall, Peter A. and David Soskice (Eds.) (2001), *Varieties of Capitalism: The Institutional Foundations of Comparative Advantage*, Oxford, England: Oxford University Press.

Hammersley, George (1991), "The effect of the technical change in the British copper industry between the 16th and the 18th centuries," *Journal of European Economic History*, 20, 155–173.

Harley, C. Knick (1982), "British industrialization before 1841: Evidence of slower growth during the Industrial Revolution," *Journal of Economic History*, 42, 267–289.

Harnack, Adolf von (1905), "Vom Großbetrieb der Wissenschaft," *Preußische Jahrbücher*, 119, 193–201.

Harrisson, Mark (Ed.) (1998), *The Economics of World War II: Six Great Powers in International Comparison*, Cambridge, England: Cambridge University Press.

Harvey, David (1989), *The Condition of Postmodernity: An Inquiry into the Origins of Cultural Change*, Oxford: Blackwell.

Haupt, Heinz-Gerhard (Ed.) (2002), *Das Ende der Zünfte: Ein europäischer Vergleich*, Kritische Studien zur Geschichtswissenschaft, vol. 151, Göttingen: Vandenhoeck.

Hegel's Philosophy of Right (1952), Translated with notes by T.M. Knox, Oxford, England: Clarendon Press.

Hertner, Peter (1986), "Financial strategies and adaption to foreign markets: The German electro-technical industry and its multinational activities, 1890s to 1939," in Alice Teichova, Maurice Leboyer, and Helga Nussbaum (Eds.), *Multinational Enterprise in Historical Perspective*, Cambridge, England: Cambridge University Press, pp. 113–134.

Hirsch, Barry; John T. Addison; and Joachim Genosko (1990), *Eine ökonomische Analyse der Gewerkschaften*, Regensburg: Transer.

Hollingsworth, J. Rogers and Robert Boyer (Eds.) 1997, *Contemporary Capitalism: The Embeddedness of Institutions*, Cambridge, England: Cambridge University Press, pp. 265–310.

Huntington, Samuel P. (1996), *The Clash of Civilizations and the Remaking of World Order*, New York: Simon & Schuster.

IFO-Institut für Wirtschaftsforschung (October 2001), "Der mittelständische Maschinenbau am Standort Deutschland—Chancen und Risiken im Zeitalter der Globalisierung und 'New Economy'," IFO-Institut für Wirtschaftsforschung, Munich.

Johnson, Jeffrey A. (2004), "The power of synthesis (1900–1925)," in Werner
Abelshauser (Ed.), *German Industry and Global Enterprise—BASF: The
History of a Company* (David Antal and Anne Stokes, Trans.), New York,
Cambridge, UK: Cambridge University Press, pp. 115–205.

Judt, Matthias and Burghard Ciesla (eds.) (1996), *Technology Transfer out of
Germany after 1945*, Amsterdam: harwood academic publishers.

Kaelble, Hartmut (1967), *Industrielle Interessenpolitik in der Wilhelminischen
Gesellschaft: Centralverband Deutscher Industrieller 1895 bis 1914*, Berlin:
Walter de Gruyter.

Kaun, Heinrich (1938), *Die Geschichte der Zentralarbeitsgemeinschaft der
industriellen und gewerblichen Arbeitgeber Deutschlands,* Jena: Gustav Fischer.

Kern, Horst and Michael Schumann (1984), *Das Ende der Arbeitsteilung?
Rationalisierung in der industriellen Produktion: Bestandsaufnahme,
Trendbestimmung*, Munich: Beck.

König, Wolfgang (2004), "Adolf Hitler vs. Henry Ford: The Volkswagen, the role of
America as a model, and the failure of a Nazi consumer society", *German
Studies Review* 27 (2), 249–268.

Kugler, Anita (1987), "Von der Werkstatt zum Fließband: Etappen der frühen
Automobilproduktion in Deutschland," *Geschichte und Gesellschaft*, 13,
304–339.

Lane, Christel (1999), "Globalization and the German model of capitalism—Erosion
or survival?" Discussion Paper, Faculty of Social and Political Science,
Cambridge University, England.

Lazonick, William (1990), *Competitive Advantage on the Shop Floor*, Cambridge,
MA: Harvard University Press.

Lessenich, Stephan (2003), Dynamischer Immobilismus, Kontinuität und Wandel im
deutschen Sozialmodell, Frankfurt am Main: Campus.

Levy, Hermann (1927), *Monopole, Kartelle und Trusts* (2nd ed.), Jena: Fischer.

Linde, Claas van der (1992), *Deutsche Wettbewerbsvorteile*, Düsseldorf: Econ.

List, Friedrich (1996), *Outlines of American Political Economy in Twelve Letters to
Charles Ingersoll*, Wiesbaden: Böttiger. (Original work published 1827)

_____ (1931), "Über den Wert und die Bedingungen einer Allianz zwischen
Großbritannien und Deutschland," in Friedrich List, *Schriften*, vol. 7. Berlin:
Reimar Hobbing, pp. 267–296. (Original work published 1846)

Maddison, Angus (1989), *The World Economy in the 20th Century*, Paris: OECD.

Maier, Charles S. (1975), *Recasting Bourgeois Europe*, Princeton: Princeton
University Press.

Manoïlesco, Mihaïl (1936), *Le siècle du corporatisme: Doctrine du corporatisme
integral et pur*, Paris: Alcan. (Original work published 1934)

Maurer, Ilse and Udo Wengst (Eds.) (1980), *Politik und Wirtschaft in der Krise
1930–1932, Quellen zur Ära Brüning,* Part 1, with an introduction by Gerhard
Schulz, Düsseldorf: Droste.

Mayer, Arno J. (1981), *The Resistence of the Old Regime: Europe to the Great War*,
New York: Pantheon.

Middlemas, Keith (1979), *Politics in Industrial Society: The Experience of the British System since 1911*, London: André Deutsch.

Mokyr, Joel (Ed.) (1993), *The British Industrial Revolution: An Economic Perspective*, Boulder, CO: Westview Press.

Mommsen, Theodor (1905), *Reden und Aufsätze*, Berlin: Weidemann.

Nolan, Mary (1994), *Visions of modernity: American Business and the Modernization of Germany*, New York: Oxford University Press.

North, Douglass C. (1981), *Structure and Change in Economic History*, New York: W. W. Norton.

_____ (1990), *Institutions, Institutional Change and Economic Performance*, Cambridge, England: Cambridge University Press.

North, Douglass C. and Robert P. Thomas (1973), *The Rise of the Western World: A New Economic History*, Cambridge, England: Cambridge University Press.

Nussbaum, Frederick L. (1933), *A History of the Economic Institutions of Modern Europe: An Introduction of* Der Moderne Kapitalismus *of Werner Sombart*, New York: F.S. Crofts & Co.

Olson, Mancur (1982), *The Rise and Decline of Nations: Economic Growth, Stagflation, and Social Rigidities*, New Haven, CT: Yale University Press.

O'Rourke, Kevin H. and Jeffrey G. Williamson (1999), *Globalization and History: The Evolution of a Nineteenth Century Atlantic Economy*, Cambridge, MA: MIT.

Orwell, George and Reginald Reynolds (Eds.) (1948), *British Pamphleteers, vol. I: From the Sixteenth Century to the French Revolution*, London: Wingate.

Pauly, Louis W. and Simon Reich (1997), "National structures and multinational corporate behavior: Enduring differences in the age of globalization," *International Organization*, 51 (1), 1–30.

Piore, Michael J. and Charles F. Sabel (1984), *The Second Industrial Divide: Possibilities for Prosperity*, New York: Basic Books.

Politische Discurs, von den eigentlichen Ursachen/deß Auff- und Abnehmens der Städt/Länder und Republicken etc (1688/1972), unchanged reprint of the 3rd ed., Glashütten im Taunus: Auvermann.

Pollard, Sidney (1970), *The Development of the British Economy, 1914–1967*, London: Arnold.

Pope Leo XIII and Pope Pius XI (1943), *On the Conditions of the Workers, and Forty Years after, on Reconstruction of Social Order*, Latin Text with English Translation, approved by the Holy See, New York and Boston: The Catholic University of America Press.

Porter, Michael E. (1990), *The Competitive Advantage of Nations*, London: The Free Press.

Ptak, Ralf (2004), *Vom Ordoliberalismus zur Sozialen Marktwirtschaft. Stationen des Neoliberalismus in Deutschland*, Opladen: Leske + Budrich.

Quinn, John Brian (1992), *Intelligent Enterprise: A Knowledge and Service Based Paradigm for Industry*, New York: The Free Press.

Rappaport, Alfred (1986), *Creating Shareholder Value: The New Standard for Business Performance*, New York: The Free Press.

Reich, Simon (1990), *The Fruits of Fascism: Postwar Prosperity in Historical Perspective*, Ithaca and London: Cornell University Press.

Rhodes, Martin and Bastiaan van Apeldoorn (1997), "Capitalism versus capitalism in western Europe," in Martin Rhodes, Paul Heywood, and Vincent Wright (Eds.), *Developments in West European Politics*, New York: St. Martin's Press, pp. 171–189.

Richta, Radovan (1971), *Richta-Report: Politische Ökonomie des 20. Jahrhunderts*, Frankfurt am Main: Makol.

Ritter, Gerhard A. and Klaus Tenfelde (1992), *Arbeiter im Deutschen Kaiserreich 1871 bis 1914*, Bonn: Dietz.

Rosenau, James N. (1990), *Turbulence in World Politics: A Theory of Change and Continuity*, New York: The Free Press.

Rosenberg, Hans (1967), *Große Depression und Bismarckzeit*, Berlin: Walter de Gruyter.

_____ (1958), Bureaucracy, Aristocracy, and Autocracy: The Prussian Experience, 1660–1815, Cambridge, MA: Harvard University Press.

Sabel, Charles F. and Jonathan Zeitlin (eds.) (1997), *World of Possibilities: Flexibility and Mass Production in Western Industrialization*, Cambridge, England, New York: Cambridge University Press.

Schmitter, Philippe C. (1974), "Still the century of corporatism?" *The Review of Politics*, 36 (1), 85–131.

_____ (1977), "Modes of interest intermediation and models of societal change in Western Europe," *Comparative Political Studies*, 10 (1), 7–38.

Schmoller, Gustav (1898), *Über einige Grundfragen der Socialpolitik und der Volkswirtschaftslehre,* Leipzig: Duncker & Humblot.

Schmoller, Gustav (1942), *The Economics of Gustav Schmoller* [Grundriss der Allgemeinen Volkswirtschaftslehre], Brooklyn, NY: Brooklyn College.

_____ (1906), "Das Verhältnis der Kartelle zum Staat" in Verein für Socialpolitik (Ed.), *Verhandlungen des Vereins für Socialpolitik am 27. und 28. September 1905 in Mannheim*, Schriften des Vereins für Socialpolitik, vol. 116, Leipzig: Duncker & Humblot, pp. 237–271.

Schumpeter, Joseph A. (1939), *Business Cycles: A Theoretical, Historical, and Statistical Analysis of the Capitalist Process*, vol. 1, New York: McGraw Hill.

Servan-Schreiber, Jean-Jacques (1968), *The American Challenge* (Ronald Steel, Trans.), London: Hamilton.

Shonfield, Andrew (1965), *Modern Capitalism: The Changing Balance of Public and Private Power*, Oxford, England: Oxford University Press.

Skidelsky, Robert (2000), *John Maynard Keynes: Fighting for Britain 1937–1946*, Basingstoke: MacMillan.

Smith, Adam (1811), *An Inquiry into the Nature and Causes of the Wealth of Nations*, vol. 1, 2nd ed. from the 11th London edition, Hartford: Oliver D. Cooke.

Smith, Toulmin (with an introductory essay by Lujo Brentano) (1870), *English Gilds*, Oxford, England: Oxford University Press.

Sombart, Werner (1955), *Das Wirtschaftsleben im Zeitalter des Hochkapitalismus*, 2nd half volume (4th ed.), Berlin: Duncker & Humblot.

Soskice, David (1999), "Divergent production regimes: Coordinated and uncoordinated market economies in the 1980s and 1990s" in Peter Lange, Herbert Kitchelt, Gary Marks, and John Stephens (Eds.), *Continuity and Change in Contemporary Capitalism*, Cambridge, England: Cambridge University Press, pp. 101–134.

Soskice, David (1999), "Globalisierung und institutionelle Divergenz: Die USA und Deutschland im Vergleich," *Geschichte und Gesellschaft*, 25, 201–225.

Ständiger Ausschuß des Vereins für Socialpolitik (Ed.) (1873), *Verhandlungen der Eisenacher Versammlung zur Besprechung der sozialen Frage*, Leipzig: Duncker & Humblot.

Stokes, Raymond G. (2004), "From the IG Farben fusion to BASF AG (1925–1952)," in Werner Abelshauser (Ed.), *German Industry and Global Enterprise—BASF: The History of a Company* (David Antal and Anne Stokes, Trans.), New York and Cambridge, England: Cambridge University Press, pp. 206–361.

Streeck, Wolfgang (1991), "On the institutional conditions of diversified quality production," in Egon Matzner and Wolfgang Streeck, *Beyond Keynesianism, The Socio-Economics of Full Employment*, Aldershot, Hants, England: Elgar, pp. 21–61.

———— (1997), "German capitalism: Does it exist? Can it survive?" in Colin Crouch and Wolfgang Streeck (Eds.), *Political Economy of Modern Capitalism: Mapping Convergence and Diversity*, London: Sage, pp. 33–54.

———— (2001), "Introduction," in Wolfgang Streeck and Kozo Yamamura (Eds.), *The Origins of nonliberal Capitalism: Germany and Japan in Comparison*, Ithaca, NY: Cornell University Press, pp. 1–38.

Streeck, Wolfgang and Norbert Kluge (Eds.) (1999), *Mitbestimmung in Deutschland: Tradition und Effizienz*, Expertenberichte für die Kommission Mitbestimmung, Bertelsmann Stiftung and Hans-Böckler-Stiftung, Frankfurt am Main and New York: Campus.

Streeck, Wolfgang and Kozo Yamamura (Eds.) (2001), *The Origins of Nonliberal Capitalism: Germany and Japan in Comparison,* Ithaca, NY: Cornell University Press.

Supple, Barry E. (1959), *Commercial Crisis and Change in England, 1600–1642: A Study in the Instability of a Mercantile Economy*, Cambridge, England: Cambridge University Press.

Taylor, Frederick Winslow (1911), *Principles of Scientific Management*, New York: Harper & Brothers.

Tilly, Richard (1999), *Globalisierung aus historischer Sicht und das Lernen aus der Geschichte*, Cologne: Forschungsinstitut für Sozial- und Wirtschaftsgeschichte an der Universität zu Köln.

Tiratsoo, Nick and Jim Tomlinson (1993), *Industrial Efficiency and State Intervention: Labour, 1939–1951*, London: Routledge.

Tocqueville, Alexis de (1966), *Democracy in America* (Henry Reeve, Trans.), vol. 1, New Rochelle, NY: Arlington House. (Original work published 1835)

Troeltsch, Ernst (1922/1965), *Die Soziallehren der christlichen Kirchen und Gruppen*, 2nd reprint, Aalen: Scientia.

Tucholsky, Kurt (1965), "Wallenstein und die Interessenten," in Fritz J. Raddatz (Ed.), *Ausgewählte Werke*, vol. 2, Reinbek bei Hamburg: Rowohlt, pp. 207–212. (Original work published 1931)

Unwin, George (1963), *The Gilds and Companies of London* (4th ed.), London: Crank Cass & Co. (Original work published 1908)

Van Hook, James C. (2004), *Rebuilding Germany: The Creation of the Social Market Economy, 1945–1957*, Cambridge, England: Cambridge University Press.

Vaudagna, Maurizio (1981), *Corporativismo e New Deal*, Turin: Rosenberg & Sellier.

Veblen, Thorstein (1968), *Imperial Germany and the Industrial Revolution*, Ann Arbor, MI: University of Michigan Press. (Original work published 1915)

Wallerstein, Immanuel (1979), *The Capitalist World-Economy*, Cambridge, England: Cambridge University Press.

Wallis, John J. and Douglass C. North (1986), "Measuring the Transaction Sector in the American Economy 1870–1970," in Stanley L. Engerman and Robert E. Gallman (Eds.), *Long-Term Factors in American Economic Growth*, Chicago: Chicago University Press, pp. 95–161.

Weber, Max (1922/1978), *Wirtschaft und Gesellschaft;* U.S. source: *Economy and Society: An Outline of Interpretive Sociology,* 2 vols., ed. by G. Roth and C. Wittich, trans. E. Fischoff, H. Gerth, A. M. Henderson, F. Kolegar, C. Wright Mills, T. Parsons, M. Rheinstein, G. Roth, E. Shils, and C. Wittich, Berkeley: University of California Press.

Wehler, Hans-Ulrich (2002), "Sonderwegsdebatte," in Michael Behnen (Ed.), *Lexikon der deutschen Geschichte 1945–1990*, Stuttgart: Kröner, pp. 531–534.

Wellhöner, Volker (1996), *"Wirtschaftswunder"—Weltmarkt—westdeutscher Fordismus: Der Fall Volkswagen*, Münster: Dampfboot.

Wengel, Jürgen and Gunter Lay (September 2001), "Deutschland und die USA auf verschiedenen Wegen: Konzepte der Produktionsmodernisierung im Vergleich" [Entire Issue], *Fraunhofer ISI, Mitteilungen aus der Produktionsinnovationserhebung*, 23.

Whiteside, Noel and Robert Salais (1997), *Governance, Industry and Labour Markets in Britain and France, 1930–1960: The Modernizing State*, London: Routledge.

Whitley, Richard (1994), "Dominant forms of economic organization in market economies," *Organization Studies*, 15 (2), 153–182.

Whitley, Richard and Peer Hull Kristensen (Eds.) (1996), *The Changing European Firm: Limits to Convergence*, London: Routledge.

Wilkins, Mira (1989), *The History of Foreign Investment in the United States to 1914*, Cambridge, MA: Harvard University Press.

Wilkins, Mira (Ed.) (1991), *The Growth of Multinationals*, Aldershot, England: Elgar.

Wilkins, Mira and Frank Ernest Hill (1964), *American Business Abroad: Ford on Six Continents*, Detroit: Wayne State University Press.

Wilkins, Mira and Harm G. Schröter (1999), *The Free-Standing Company in the World Economy, 1830–1996*, Oxford: Oxford University Press.

Williamson, Jeffrey G. (1984), "Why was British growth so slow during the Industrial Revolution?" *Journal of Economic History*, 44, 687–712.

Williamson, Oliver E. (1985), *The Economic Institutions of Capitalism: Firms, Markets, Relational Contracting*, New York: The Free Press.

Wrigley, Edward A. (1988), *Continuity, Chance and Change: The Character of the Industrial Revolution in England*, Cambridge, England: Cambridge University Press.

Zeitlin, Jonathan and Gary Herrigel (Eds.) (2000), *Americanization and Its Limits: Reworking US Technology and Management in Post-war Europe and Japan*, Oxford, England, and New York: Oxford University Press.

Zilbert, Edward R. (1981), *Albert Speer and the Nazi Ministry of Arms: Economic Institutions and Industrial Production in the German War Economy*, London: Associated University Presses.

Subject Index